When the Members are the Missionaries

An Extraordinary
Calling for
Ordinary People

A. Wayne Schwab

Prologue by Jürgen Moltmann
Foreword by Ian T. Douglas

Member Mission Press
Essex, New York

ISBN 0-9717552-0-5

Library of Congress Control Number 2002004606

When the Members are the Missionaries:
An Extraordinary Calling for Ordinary People
First Member Mission Press Edition 2002, Essex, NY 12936

Cover design by Media Graphics, Inc.

Copies may be ordered from:

Member Mission Press
P.O. Box 308
Essex, New York 12936

www.membermissionpress.org

This book was made possible, in part, through grant support from Trinity Grants Program, Trinity Church, New York for a project in Missionary Spirituality.

Dedicated to:

All who seek to bring good news in deed and word
wherever they are, all the time.

CONTENTS

FOREWORD

Ian T. Douglas

Talk of mission seems to be gaining ground in church circles, particularly within some corners of what have been considered "mainline" Protestant churches in the United States. The cynical amongst us would say that mission-talk represents the newest attempt of American Protestants to reassert power previously afforded to us by Christendom, an attempt to reverse the slide from mainline to sideline status. For such folk, mission and mission-talk become the backdrop for the next strategic plan, whose real agenda is to fill the pews once again and secure the budgets of the parish and judicatories. The oft heard call "to move from maintenance to mission," if scrutinized closely, seldom challenges the implicit structures and ecclesiologies of most American Protestant churches. Rather, mission becomes, as Bishop Stephen F. Bayne once said: "a way of keeping God in business" (E. R. Fairweather, ed., *Anglican Congress 1963: Report of the Proceedings*, Toronto: Editorial Committee of the Anglican Congress, 1963, 130). Johannes Hoekendijk, a contemporary of Bayne, put it another way. "The call to evangelism is often little else than a call to restore 'Christendom,' the *Corpus Christianum*, as a solid well-integrated cultural complex, directed and dominated by the Church. And the sense of urgency is often nothing but a nervous feeling of insecurity, with the established Church endangered; a flurried activity to save the remnants of a time now irrevocably past (Johannes C. Hoekendijk, "The Call to Evangelism," International Review of Missions 39, April 1950: 163).

Hoekendijk argued that "Evangelization and *churchification* are not identical, and very often they are each other's bitterest enemies"(Ibid., 171). He wanted to move mission from an ecclesiological to an eschatological point of departure. For him, the goal of evangelism, the goal of mission, was not to extend the Church as the *Corpus Christianum* but rather to participate with God in God's new creation, to work for God's *Shalom*. Hoekendijk was the first of his generation to suggest that it was

God's mission in the world to bring about God's *Shalom*, God's Kingdom, God's Reign.

Missiologists, those who study and write about the theology of Christian mission, affirm that the mission of God, the *missio Dei*, is God's action in the world to bring about God's Reign. The Trinitarian God, Creator, Redeemer, and Sanctifier, has effected a new order, a new *Shalom*; one in which all of creation can find new life and new hope in and with God. Unlike the early proponents of the *missio Dei* who eschewed the role of the Church in God's mission, contemporary mission thinkers affirm that the Church, as the Body of Christ in the world, does have a central role to play in the salvific work of God. David J. Bosch's magisterial review of biblical, historical, and theological perspectives on mission, *Transforming Mission: Paradigm Shifts in Theology of Mission* (Maryknoll, NY: Orbis Books, 1991), traces this important development in mission thought. Bosch and other contemporary mission thinkers affirm that the Church is called and uniquely empowered by the Holy Spirit to participate with God in God's mission of reconciliation, redemption, and liberation to the ends of the earth — and at home!

Over the past two decades some missiologists have begun to turn their attention to gospel and culture questions and the role of the Church in God's mission within our own North American context. Challenged by the writings of the great English missionary and bishop to South India, Lesslie Newbigin, especially his books: *The Open Secret: Sketches for a Missionary Theology* (1978), *Foolishness to the Greeks: The Gospel and Western Culture* (1986), and *The Gospel in a Pluralist Society* (1989), scholars and church leaders are asking hard questions about the missionary vocation of the Church in North America. One group in particular, The Gospel and Our Culture Network, (www.gocn.org) is asking hard questions about what God's mission might look like here in the post-Christendom, post-modern context of the United States. Network participants such as Lois Barrett, Inagrace T. Dietterich, Darrell Guder, George Hunsberger, Alan J. Roxburgh, and Craig Van Gelder are challenging Christians in North America to free themselves from old structures and old ways of being Church in order to be sent anew in God's mission here at home. (See the series of books produced by the Gospel and Our Culture network and published by Eerdmans, particularly: Darrell L. Guder, ed., *Missional Church: A Vision for the Sending of the Church in North America, The Gospel and Our Culture Series,* Grand Rapids, Michigan: William B. Eerdmans, 1998).

This book by A. Wayne Schwab, although not directly linked to the Gospel in Our Culture Network, shares many of the presuppositions and theological constructs of the contemporary missiologists writing about the Church in North America. Schwab, the first evangelism staff officer for the Episcopal Church in the United States, has a love of the Church and is writing for those who find themselves to be part of the Body of Christ in these exciting and challenging times in North America. As much as Schwab loves the Church, he loves God's mission more. His aim in this book is to empower and energize the baptized to reclaim their central role in God's mission. As the *laos*, the people of God, claim their place in God's mission, the world — and the Church — will discover the Good News of God in Christ for this time and place.

While Schwab stands on the shoulders of Hoekendijk, Newbigin, Bosch, and the Gospel in our Culture Network missiologists, he also stands within the missiological and methodological tradition of the Episcopal Church and wider Anglicanism.

The in-breaking of God's new creation, God's *Shalom*, at the heart of the *missio Dei*, is consistent with the Episcopal Church's articulated vocation to participate with God in mending the brokenness of creation and healing the rift between humanity, nature, and God. In the Catechism or "Outline of the Faith" found in the back of *The Book of Common Prayer* (New York: The Church Hymnal Corporation, 1979, p. 855), the question is asked: "What is the mission of the Church?" The answer given is: "The mission of the Church is to restore all people to unity with God and each other in Christ." Despite the ecclesiocentrism of this missiological affirmation, the *missio Dei* underpinnings of this statement cannot be denied. The Episcopal Church has gone on record that the mission of God, as manifested in the Church as the Body of Christ, is no less than the eschatological restoration of all people to unity with God and each other in Christ. But the Catechism does not stop here. It further asks through whom does the Church carry out its mission (God's mission)? The response: "The Church carries out its mission through the ministry of all its members (Ibid.)." In other words, the baptized are the missionaries.

The affirmation that all the baptized are missionaries is not new for the Episcopal Church. For more than a century and a half, the Episcopal Church has affirmed that baptism incorporates the faithful into the mission of God. The 1835 General Convention of the Protestant Episcopal Church in the United States, in the new constitution to the Church's Domestic and Foreign Missionary Society, proclaimed boldly that all

Episcopalians, by virtue of baptism and not voluntary association, were to be members of the missionary society. Put another way, the Church was to be coterminous with the missionary society; mission and the Church are inextricably linked. With the development of a centralized national program of education, social service, and missions in 1919, the Domestic and Foreign Missionary Society became the incorporated appellation for the new "national church" structure. Today the name remains the legal title for the corporate work of the Episcopal Church in the United States. The Episcopal Church is thus first and foremost a missionary society and participation in God's mission is at the heart of the baptismal call. Baptism is a commission, co-mission, in God's mission. Just as God sent Jesus into the world, and Jesus sent his disciples to the ends of the earth, we too are sent in mission as the Body of Christ in the world today. The imperative and the mandate are clear: the members are the missionaries.

As much as Schwab affirms the missiological tradition of the Episcopal Church he also demonstrates his embrace of Anglican theological method in the style and examples used in the book. Given the truth that has flowed from the reality of the life, death, and resurrection of Jesus Christ, Anglicans might be accused of an over affinity for the doctrine of the incarnation. In the incarnation of God in Jesus, God joined the human family in all of our sinfulness and all of our possibility. Anglican emphasis on the incarnation affirms that the truth of God in Christ is continually revealed to the Church and the world through scripture, reason, and tradition. God is made known in the real life, flesh and blood, working out of our lives, as individuals and in community. Anglican theological method is thus grounded in the affirmation of the human story as God's story.

Schwab thus opens this work with story, or more specifically, fifteen stories of baptized Christians pursuing God's mission, at home and at work, in the local community and the wider world, in leisure, and in the Church. Beginning with real life stories to demonstrate and emphasize that the members are the missionaries is a profoundly Anglican way of doing business. Instead of starting with some set of *a priori* truth claims about mission, Schwab grounds his missiological thought in the experiences of Kit, Jim, Mary Ann, Robbie, and eleven other individuals. Only after telling their truths as missionaries does Schwab begin to sketch out how to organize a congregation around mission. Schwab's seeking the truth of the incarnation as it is known in the truths of the lives of the baptized growing together as the Body of Christ in the world today characterizes the best of Anglican theological method while enlivening missiological reflection in the United States.

I highly commend Wayne Schwab's *When the Members are the Missionaries*. Its wonderful stories, insightful analysis, and practical suggestions will contribute greatly to both missiological and congregational development literature for the contemporary North American context. Faithful worshipers and parish members, pastors, church leaders, and judicatory executives, as well as seminary students and teachers, will all find something rewarding and challenging in these pages. God willing, the book will help Episcopalians and others to own the baptismal call to become missionaries and in so doing move the Church in the United States from ecclesial maintenance to genuine participation in God's mission.

Ian T. Douglas
Professor of World Mission and Global Christianity
Episcopal Divinity School
Cambridge, Massachusetts

ACKNOWLEDGMENTS

This book could never have appeared without a legion of helpers — remote and immediate. Among the immediate helpers are the following people:

The fifteen missionaries, anonymous for the most part, whose readiness to tell of their missions and themselves made this book possible — and make the book itself.

Then come those dedicated people who labored through the first draft in whole or in part to make their invaluable comments from their particular fields of expertise:

John E. Ambelang, Rector of St. Francis' Episcopal Church, Menomonee Falls, Wisconsin;

James D. Anderson, retired author and consultant in congregational development;

Daniel T. Benedict Jr., author and Worship Resources Director, General Board of Discipleship, United Methodist Church;

Mary Ann Brody, lay leader and middle school science teacher, now a student at a theological seminary;

Donna B. Cosulich, lay leader and retired chemist;

Ian T. Douglas, World Mission and Global Christianity, Episcopal Divinity School for background in the *missio Dei*;

Ransom Duncan, lay leader and retired technical director for a food manufacturer;

Ralph E. East, student, for help with graphics;

Jerrold Hames, editor, *Episcopal Life*;

John W. B. Hill, Incumbent, St. Augustine of Canterbury, Toronto, Canada, author, liturgist, and leader in catechumenal formation;

Robert D. Hofstad, Bishop of the Southwestern Washington Synod of the Evangelical Lutheran Church of America;

Sheryl Kujawa, Director of Congregational Studies and Associate Professor of Pastoral Theology, Episcopal Divinity School;

Anthony L'Esperance, artist, photographer, and manufacturer;

Mary S. Martin, Rector, St. John's Episcopal Church, San Bernardino, California;

George L. Peabody, Systems Consultant, skills for change and leadership;

James M. Perry, Steward of Appointed Leadership, Minnesota Annual Conference, United Methodist Church;

Timothy F. Sedgwick, Professor of Christian Ethics, Virginia Theological Seminary; and

Karen M. Ward, Associate Director for Worship, Evangelical Lutheran Church in America.

Some guides, before as well as during the preparation were as follows:

W. Warner Burke, organization consultant, who introduced me to Abraham Zaleznik and leader vs. manager roles;

Louis Weil, now James F. Hodges Professor of Liturgics, Church Divinity School of the Pacific, who guided my writing and action research in catechumenal formation;

Verna Dozier, author and teacher, who inspired me to continue during the planning stages;

Ezra Earl Jones, past General Secretary, General Board of Discipleship, United Methodist Church, who widened my understanding of church systems at all levels;

Shawn McDermott and the staff of the Bishop Payne Library, Virginia Theological Seminary, who were always ready to help with research.

And appreciation extends to Missionary Spirituality Project teammates: Glen F. Michaels, past Rector of St. John's Episcopal Church, Essex, New York, and Juan M. C. Oliver, now Director, George Mercer Memorial School of Theology, Garden City, New York; Clayton L. Morris, Liturgical Officer, Episcopal Church Center, who offered approaches in liturgy; Theological consultants: J. M. Mark Dyer, Professor of Theology and Director of Spiritual Formation at the Virginia Theological Seminary and Anglican Co-chair of the International Commission of the Anglican-Orthodox Theological Dialogue; David A. Scott, Professor of Systematic Theology and Ethics, Virginia Theological Seminary; and James A. Carpenter, retired Professor of Systematic Theology, General Theological Seminary.

A grant from the Trinity Grants Program (Trinity Church, New York City, New York) funded a project in Missionary Spirituality, which has led to this book.

My competent, patient, and consistently supportive project editor was Irene V. Jackson-Brown.

The most consistent help and encouragement continues to come from my wife, Betty.

A Wayne Schwab
Essex, New York

PREFACE

A. Wayne Schwab

Where do you look to see what a congregation looks like when its members are the missionaries? Do not look at the congregation. Look at the members. Look at what they are doing in their daily lives. Part One introduces you to the vision of the members as the missionaries and tells the stories of fifteen missionaries. Part Two is a manual for reorganizing a congregation around this vision.

Six and a half years into retirement I am still learning about my own missions. Training hands, head, and heart for the mission is a lifelong task. For me, that included twenty years leading congregations and almost nineteen years as the Episcopal Church's first-ever national staff person for evangelism. In many ways, I had to be free of church employment before I could get free of the church to discover the mission. For whom is this book written? While for clergy and lay leaders primarily, it is for anyone who is on the journey to a heart and a head for the mission.

This book deals with more than growing the congregation and running it well. It offers ways to help members live better as Christians Monday to Monday — to be missionaries, not just members of a congregation. I pray that all readers, encounter a challenging vision. Clergy who embrace this vision will be in the best position to make it a reality. Lay leaders who share the vision will be strong allies for these clergy. Bishops may well catch the vision, too. Bishops can do the most to realize it. They can begin to focus the interests, activities, and resources of their dioceses on this vision. Seminarians start at the beginning. They can integrate all they learn, talk about, and wrestle with into this vision. The integration will be lifelong, but they may have the least to unlearn.

Where laity find no interest in this book's approach to mission in their clergy or among other members, the stories in the first part of the book may offer them sufficient help to find and to live their missions on their own. This observation came from one of my readers — a lay person.

I am indebted to the traditional Anglican emphasis on the incarnation. God is at work among us, supremely in Jesus Christ. My approach is more experiential than academic. Deed and word are inseparable. So, Part One is stories of the baptized in daily life. And Part Two is how to reshape a congregation to support the baptized in their daily living. Anglicanism also works from the experience of worshiping believers. Worship rather than a confessional statement is our anchor. "As we pray, so we believe" and so we live. While typically Anglican, Anglicanism has no monopoly on this approach.

I hope that members of other communions will find this book useful. Since I am rooted in this tradition, the book had to be written out of what I know. However, this book would not have been brought to life without the help of members of other communions. Therefore, I hope that readers from other communions will find enough common ground for it to be useful.

Details of all the above come out, I pray, in the following pages. What you find here are the fruits of some rich experiences in mission: theological education at Virginia Theological Seminary, 1950-53; a year selling Fuller Brush products, after seminary, and serving as a church's young adult adviser; meeting and marrying Betty; two years as an assistant rector in Washington, D.C.; nineteen years as rector of St. Paul's Church, Montvale, New Jersey; trainee and then a leadership team member in the Episcopal Church's work in education and leadership development; work with the Department of the Laity of the World Council of Churches; church and secular experience as an organization development consultant using community development approaches from Europe's lay academies; experience as a certified pastoral counselor; nineteen years as the first evangelism staff person for the Episcopal Church; working in this field in Central America, Canada, the Philippines, and Spain; after retirement in 1993, as a consultant to the Evangelism Working Group of the National Council of Churches of Christ; interim work in a small upstate New York congregation; work on the Missionary Spirituality project on the daily missions of church members; community service in school and government; and marriage and family life with two sons and two daughters since 1954.

As for the text itself, quotation marks indicate the words of the missionaries themselves. All biblical quotations are taken from the *New Revised Standard Version*.

PROLOGUE

Jürgen Moltmann

Professor Moltmann's comments were made during a conversation with the author on September 4, 2001, in Tübingen, Germany.

I am interested especially in the case studies and also in the idea — the member as missionary. So, I would like to endorse your restoration of mission.

The book is not a case for specialists. It makes the claim for the generalist — every Christian, every Christian is a missionary.

I think it is important to say this again and again because we like to delegate things to specialists.

As a Christian, I delegate my worship to the pastor; my diaconic duties to the deacon; my management to the manager; my teeth to the dentist; and so everything is delegated and then I am empty and lonely. That is not good.

So, to me, delegation always means alienation. I am alienated from myself.

To rediscover that I can do all these things in my own way would be great for the normal Christian person.

Pentecostals know that and they tell you that you can do all these things. And they expect you to do them in your way.

Since his first book, Theology of Hope, in 1965, Jürgen Moltmann, Emeritus Professor of Theology at the University of Tübingen in Germany, has written continuously about the issues facing Christians and the world as a whole. When he was a despairing prisoner of war from 1945-48, he found his way to faith when he read the passage, "My God, my God why have you forsaken me?" in a Bible given him by an American military chaplain.

PART ONE

Stories of the Missionaries

". . . I was not disobedient to the heavenly vision . . ."
(Acts 26:19)

Chapter 1 — The Vision: When the Members are the Missionaries

The essential place of the laity

In 1958 in *A Theology of the Laity*, Hendrik Kraemer excited Christians with a vision of the essential place of the laity in the church. "If the laity of the Church, dispersed in and through the world, are really what they are called to be, the real uninterrupted dialogue between Church and world happens through them. They form the daily repeated projections of the Church into the world. They embody the meeting of Church and World" (Westminster, 1958, p. 170).

Kraemer's vision is still unrealized. The laity are not central because the mission is not central. We say the church has a mission. We get it wrong when we talk that way. The truth is the mission has a church. When mission becomes central, the laity become central.

Who are the laity? All of the baptized who have two tasks wherever they are: one, to transform the world to accord with God's reign of love and justice; and two, to make known the one in whose name and by whose power we act, Jesus Christ. Deed and word, transformation and proclamation — these are the stuff of missionaries, the agents of mission who live *in the world*, the place of "bearing fruit" as Jesus' people.

To be sure, corporate and private worship and Christian community are the "heartland" (see p. 111) of each Christian. They are the wells from which we drink and never thirst. Still, daily life is where the world meets us. Daily life is where what we believe and how we choose to live takes on flesh in behalf of others. For too long, congregations have ignored looking at how their members live. How their members live is the real measure of the effectiveness of a congregation.

Congregations can help their members to be better missionaries, even small congregations of fewer than fifty. In April 1999, twenty-two small congregations finished a year trying to help their members to be better missionaries. Some were urban, others suburban in New Jersey, New York,

Minnesota, California, and Alaska. One of the congregations, St. John's, Essex, New York, sponsored a grant from Trinity Church, New York City, to fund the work.

The project was named "Missionary Spirituality." I first found this term in Brian Farran's writing on the qualities of effective congregations in Western Australia in the *Anglican Theological Review*, Fall 1996. I found it even more apt for effective Christians. The words pointed to a Christian whose spirituality was based on mission. The arenas of daily life were the mission fields, and relationship with God supplied the direction and power for life there. The twenty-two congregations did not discover "just how to do it," but they did discover some of the basic questions to ask. This book explores those questions.

Mission: living and talking good news

"Mission" is the Christian story. Who has not traced the "missionary journeys" of St. Paul? Who has not seen the expansion of the church as mission in response to the Great Commission of Matthew 28:18-20? Mission has come to mean transforming the world in Jesus Christ's name as well as preaching Jesus Christ with transformation of the individual called for in both personal and public living.

John Macquarrie in *Principles of Christian Theology*, 1977, links mission and the kingdom of God. Its end is "the kingdom of God, an all-embracing commonwealth of love and freedom, in which all humanity — and indeed all creation — will be renovated and transformed" (pp. 441-2). He notes that "ministry" and "mission" draw attention to different aspects of the same phenomenon of the movement from creation to the consummation of the kingdom of God. Macquarrie also links mission and ministry as the same work. Mission is ministry in its "outgoing and expanding aspect" (p. 420).

"An Outline of the Faith" of the *Book of Common Prayer* (Church Publishing, 1979) has three questions on mission (p. 855). They appear to unite word and deed in their central use of verbs in "restore," "proclaims," and "promotes," ending with "carries out its mission through the ministry of all its members."

At its 1997 General Convention in Philadelphia, the Episcopal Church approved the Episcopal Partnership for Global Mission. Its "Theological Affirmations" conclude with these words: "As missionaries, Christians are nourished by God's Word and sacraments, and sent into the world in God's name to bring hope, healing, and justice to a sinful, divided, and broken world." These words echo a conviction that appeared as early as the 1820s and 1830s among Episcopal leaders. Ian T. Douglas in *Fling Out the Banner: The National Church Ideal and the Foreign Mission of the Episcopal Church* (Church Hymnal Corporation, 1996) has demonstrated that they already sensed something of today's recovery of mission as the call of each of the baptized. Until then, missionary societies were voluntary. In 1835, the General Convention chose The Domestic and Foreign Missionary Society as its official name. Mission was now the responsibility of every member. Mission was the work of all, not just those who volunteered for it. This was a significant shift in identity. All the baptized are missionaries and the whole world is the field of mission — home as well as beyond our borders.

The 1835 Convention elected Jackson Kemper as the Episcopal Church's first "missionary bishop" to form dioceses where none existed in Missouri and Indiana. Kemper went in the name of the whole church, not just a voluntary society of some of its members. Preaching at Kemper's consecration in 1835, G. W. Doane said, "She [the Episcopal Church] is to be a *Missionary Church* . . . Her *members*, baptized into the death of Jesus, and so purchased by His blood, are *Missionaries* all, in spirit and intent" (*Documents of Witness*, Church hymnal Corporation, 1994; the italics represent Doane's own handwritten emphasis). Summarizing the breakthrough of 1835, Douglas comments, "To be an Episcopalian is to be involved in mission. The church is mission (p. 35)." These leaders were anticipating what has come to be known as the *missio Dei* in the second half of the twentieth century (see p. 105). This book is not a departure from the past but a continuation of a vision we have been about for a long time.

The mission, then, is to live and to talk the good news. What is the good news? Through Jesus Christ, God overcomes evil, sin, and death and works to bring the whole creation to fulfillment in the Holy Spirit. God calls us to love all people, to seek justice for all people, and to talk with all people of what God is doing in Jesus Christ. The mission unites *both* word *and* deed. Our mission in every arena of daily life is to witness in deed and word to the good news of what God has done for us in Jesus Christ. These arenas are our homes, our workplaces, our communities, the wider world, our leisure, and our church life.

A fresh look at mission fields and mission

Mark Gibbs, a leader in the rediscovery of the missions of each of the baptized, names five arenas of daily life as mission fields — home, work, the local community, the wider world (beyond the local community), and leisure. As the world advances, leisure has become an industry, and our free time has become an ever more critical mission field. What about our leisure? Does our leisure indulge us or recreate us? I add a sixth mission field — the faith community, where our faith assumptions are shared. Everyone, Christian and non-Christian alike, lives in these six arenas. Even atheists with their confidence in their own powers of analysis and will to achieve hold this confidence in faith. They have a faith community of their own. At any given moment, in each of these arenas, each of us pursues some kind of specific objective or goal or mission. What we work for in each arena of our daily lives is a mission.

Each mission has three dimensions. One, a mission is specific. Two, a mission includes both direct and implied tasks to achieve it. Three, a mission is discerned as what God is calling one to do, to be, or to change. One believes one "is charged" by God with the mission one pursues at a given moment in a given arena. "Belief" is the key word. The mission I discern is discerned in faith. Since missions are specific, their duration can be as short as one week or as long as several years.

In this study, a missionary is responsible for both deeds and words, both acting and talking. Christian mission involves *both* deeds of love *and* justice and words pointing to their source in God's reign in Jesus Christ. *The Book of Common Prayer* calls for proclaiming the gospel both "by word and example." Further, the "missionary," the agent of the mission, is so often thought to be the ordained person. It is time for all the baptized to claim that grand role. How much more exciting Christian living becomes when each of the baptized begins to see each arena of her or his daily life as a "mission field" and her or his role there as the role of a missionary!

Not an original vision

While the early Christians may not have talked of "missions" and "mission fields" in this way, present among them was the same vision of themselves as agents of Jesus Christ wherever they were all the time. The vision of the members as the missionaries took on flesh in its own way when Jesus sent out the twelve, and then the seventy, to preach and to heal (Mark 6:7-13). Paul reminded Jesus' people in Corinth, " . . . we are ambassadors for Christ . . . "(2 Cor 5:20a). What early Christians knew to be "church" is a far cry from what we have now. Maintaining the institution far outweighs the mission today. Many are working to redress this imbalance. We are going through a second reformation as many reexamine what we are about and refocus on a vision based in mission. May this book be part of the next step in this direction.

God's mission and our missions

It is time to move beyond speaking of mission as only the works of a congregation, a diocese, or a communion such as a food shelf, a senior housing facility, or a healing and teaching ministry in a non-Christian nation. A retiree working to prevent gambling in his state is on a mission. A vacation Bible school leader pursues a mission as she helps the partici-pants to get along better with one another. Another is on a mission when she pursues quiet time in order to be a better parent and spouse. Mission has been the grand word for what the church gathered does. But, mem-bers can also claim that word when they seek to bring good news in deed and word to some specific need in daily life.

The theological basis for using "mission" and "missionary" this way is that the mission is God's mission to bring the creation to fulfillment. The church and its baptized members participate in God's mission in and through Jesus Christ. While we are not the exclusive bearers of God's mis-sion, we have a role to play in it. What we do in our daily arenas are the means by which we participate in God's mission as agents of Jesus Christ. We are "missionaries" in our daily arenas because we have been incorpo-rated into God's mission by baptism. Our daily arenas are "mission fields" as places where God is already on mission and we seek to join God's work there. In all, what we undertake are "missions" only because they partici-pate in God's mission.

A Lutheran colleague tells me that Martin Luther talked of the specific daily tasks of Christians as their "offices" as they live out their Christian baptismal calling or "vocation." Plumber, mother, son, spouse, Sunday school teacher, Little League coach, judge, and state senator are "offices." Then, one can more easily see mission occur in the state senate, or court-room, or under someone's sink. In these offices, we sometimes honor voca-tion and sometimes we dishonor it.

Beware sliding into a nineteenth century understanding of mission and missionary. At that time, it was hard to distinguish mission from colonial-ism and imperialism. Too often, mission included imposing the particular church, cultural, economic, or political forms of one people on another. "Mission" was "ours to do out there for them who do not have what we have." The "missionary" was one who went "out there to take them what

5

only we have." For many, mission continues to be a bad word. It is time to recover mission and missionary as *good* words.

Beware also of an individualistic understanding of missionary. The missionary is never the "rugged individualist" of a John Ford western. First, the missionary can carry on the mission only because he or she is rooted in a vital community with other missionaries. Second, the missionary always looks for people in the place of the mission to join him or her in the mission. Third, there is an aloneness to the work of the missionary. So often, the Christian is the only one asking what is God doing in this place and seeking to join God's work there. This isolation would be unbearable without living with the "communion of the saints." The lonely missionary draws courage by seeing, with the eye of faith, that he or she is surrounded and upheld by "a great cloud of witnesses." Sustained in this way, the missionary is opened by the loneliness to understand something of what Jesus' own mission was like in its radical isolation.

Note too that while there are other and time-honored words for the baptized Christian, they lack the unique connotations of "missionary." "Disciple," as commonly used, tends to point to following more than to leading in change. "Apostle" tends to point to authority — as in "the apostles' teaching and fellowship" (*Book of Common Prayer*, 1979, p. 304) — rather than to the missionary's skill for dialogue. In its emphasis on service, "minister" can miss the assertiveness needed by the missionary.

Among many Christians, "missionary" is still a revered word. May this book's use of the word speed its recovery by all Christians. Readers may find a second look at the Preface and Foreword useful at this point.

Interestingly, as I talk with people on the fringe or outside the church, I find that "missionary" never became a "bad" word for them. Apparently, many do not know of the nineteenth century abuses of mixing faith and colonialism. Recovering mission and missionary as good words may not be as hard as it looks.

Our missions are sacramental

Sacraments are means God uses to act in our lives. A colleague in baptismal liturgy and formation, John W. B. Hill, reminds me that seeing our missions as sacramental can help us in a variety of ways. We often struggle with a sense that God is distant and removed from us. Sacramental thinking reminds us that God customarily works through the things of this world. That includes our missions and those onerous, grubby parts of any mission. Jesus had to do the dishes and to seek constantly for new ways to phrase his message. Having to repeat some dull task still one more time — whether it is recycling glass bottles and tin cans or cleaning up the house or cleaning up the hard drive of our computer — is transformed when seen as part of God's sacramental work in this world. Finally, sacramental thinking can deliver us from feeling burdened by still one more demand. We already have more than we can handle. Our plates are too full. Sacramental thinking does not ask us to do more but to see what we are doing now differently; see what we are doing in the larger setting of God's ongoing work to hold life together and to bring it to ultimate fulfillment. God does not tire of the work and can give us energy to carry on. God is at work with us now in the missions already on our plates.

Real, not perfect

What does a congregation look like when the members are the missionaries? To describe times the church is gathered is to miss the radical changes made when the members are the missionaries. The accurate answer lies in what the members are doing in their daily lives. So we will capture accounts of the present missions of some real missionaries. As you read, you will not meet perfect people. You will meet real people.

You may want to know how these stories were collected. The criteria for selecting a missionary were: (1) acting in the particular mission field out of belief that she or he is doing the Lord's work there; and (2) having "both feet in the church." By the second, I mean one who shares in the bread and wine regularly and who, for all its faults, values the church. To find these missionaries, I went to laity and clergy whom I had met in the congregations participating in the Missionary Spirituality project. Actual names and places are not used in the stories for the most part. Where specifics are found, the nature of the story called for them.

As noted above, the project's purpose was to discover how small congregations could help their members to be better missionaries. Trios of a clergy person and two laity from each congregation met for three days of orientation to start the project. During the following year, we shared ideas and experiences through e-mail. The same group met again at the end of the year to draft what we had learned and what next steps might be. This book summarizes those learnings and points to next steps to make them part of congregational life.

The laity whose stories appear here became visible through what they shared during the project. When I needed to go beyond the laity I had met, I went to the clergy of these congregations and gave them my two criteria. Several times I was referred to people beyond their congregations whom they knew well. I found that many of the clergy had difficulty finding members who met the two criteria. To me, this was a sign of how far we have strayed from the laity having a sense of serving God in their daily living.

All the stories come from what people are already doing. While the stories may not be as exciting as the Damascus road was for Paul (Acts 9:1-9), they are the real stuff of everyday life. Such down to earth activities are often glossed over by church leaders. Yet, they are very real and loaded with meaning and emotion for ordinary people. Read through them with care and they will probably make you a better listener, as they did me. The descriptions of the missions and of the people themselves vary in content and length. What may seem unnecessary or insignificant was important to the teller. These apparently insignificant incidents are incidents that God has used to prepare people for their missions. Also, some missionaries are terse in talking about themselves. Others want to share their full story. All need careful listening. Finally, each person interviewed responded easily and quickly when asked for the basics of his or her faith and ethics and where he or she learned them. Evidently, seeking to live as missionaries leads people to think through the basics of their ethics and faith.

As you read, notice where, at a crucial time, each person was touched by a church member or the congregation as a whole in some meaningful way. That "touch" led, finally, to the mission you are reading about. Play these incidents the other way and you will discover the things church people and congregations do or do not do that turn people away — or never, even, reach them. Suppose St. John's in San Bernardino had not bothered to feed the poor. Susan would never have seen the newspaper picture that drew her out of her lapsed state back into church life and, finally, led to her mission in community rehabilitation. Suppose the aggressive church developer had not asserted himself to get pre-teen Roy and his brothers into Sunday School. The pastor could easily have said to himself, "If their parents don't do anything, why should I bail them out!" Roy would, probably, never have gotten that early start in spirituality that, eventually, bore fruit in leading a church-based fly tying group.

Along the way, let me note that, while developing this book, I am living a story of my own that, I believe, merits inclusion. While this may seem unusual, two reasons led me to do so. First, I needed to experience what I was asking others to do — that is, to put into print one of my own missions and something of my own journey in faith. Second, my wife and I are concerned that we hear of so many married retirees who seem to live more as married singles than as couples still growing together. Thus, my decision to tell this story, too.

As you read the stories themselves, read them as if you were actually listening to the other person. On the first reading, you may want to concentrate on the specific missions that come first in each story. If so, do return to read the rest of each missionary's story for a fuller appreciation of the depth of their commitment to mission. Also, on the first reading, you may want to read just those stories that catch your interest. There are two stories in each mission field — one about a man, the other about a woman. The mission field of home has four stories because it is so central, yet so varied today. The mission field of work has three stories to include the role of a supervisor.

Working by phone, I talked with all the people, describing the way I would use their story and, with their consent, I sent them the questions for that daily arena. I adapted the specific wording of the questions to the actual mission each person was carrying on. As their responses came in, I began to see a place for more information about the people themselves. Knowing more about the people and their pilgrimages would increase appreciation of their missions.

Still working by phone, I followed up with these questions.

1. For a brief biography: Who is at home with you now? Do you have any sons or daughters? What are their ages? Where are they now? What is your work situation? and What background do you have in church life?

2. Not all of us have been in the church all our lives; how did you come to participate in worship and church life at the present time?

3. What are some of the basics of your faith? How did you learn them? How did you learn to connect them with daily life?

4. What are some of the basics of your ethics? How did you learn them? How did you learn to connect them with daily life?

Their fuller life stories highlight the long conditioning needed to make a missionary. Highlighted, also, are the elementary events that mark turning points in the faith journey of some and intense encounters with God for others. Highlighted by all is the implied serious religious quest of every human being.

Perceiving the full scope of our daily missions

As I collected the stories of mission that follow, I was guided by a series of questions I picked up from work with Jim Anderson. We were working with retirees to discover missions that might give their retirement years excitement and purpose. Research had shown the well-being of retirees was greatly enhanced when they were spending themselves in a mission of some kind. We used a series of questions to help the retirees find meaningful missions. In an expanded form, I found the questions valued by Christians of all ages. I have used the questions in workshops to help people to discover tasks or missions in their daily arenas for the first time. Again, I have used the questions to help people already deep into their missions to see dimensions they had overlooked. I also encourage people to remember that environmental issues arise in each of our mission fields.

In general terms, these seven questions follow. Use the alternate wording as desired. After each question, I have noted the assumptions that underlie it.

1. What has God been telling me or doing through my life in this mission field?

   Assumption: God is already present and at work in each of one's mission fields. All mission is part of God's mission. Mission is God's work in which we share. (See p. 105 for more on this concept of the mission of God, *missio Dei*.)

2. What conditions inhibit reconciliation, justice, and love (peacemaking, fairness, and caring) in this mission field?

   Assumption: God's characteristic works are reconciliation, justice, and love. Hence, to begin to discern what God is already doing, look for what is blocking God's characteristic works. These will be places where God is already working for change.

3. What change is needed to increase reconciliation, justice, and love (peacemaking, fairness, and caring) in this mission field?

   Assumption: The Holy Spirit works to align the Christian's discernment of what is needed with what God is already doing. This question draws on the unique being of each Christian. Two parents in the same home will probably discern different needed changes. Two workers in the same workplace will probably discern different needed changes.

4. What will I do to achieve this change considering my gifts, limitations, and convictions?

Assumption: One draws on what one brings to the situation. While growth into some new direction may well be called for, that new direction will be a logical next step in the Christian's growth.

5. What vision (description of what I will do) will I use to draw others into working with me for this change?

Assumption: The Christian needs at least one person, but preferably a team, to share the mission. The Christian's companion or team may not share the Christian faith so a vision should be worded in non-theological language and worded in a way that stimulates desire to work for it.

6. How will I talk of God while I am sharing my vision (what I plan to do) or following through on it?

Assumption: Rephrase the vision in explicit theological language to describe how God is at work in it. Without explicit talk of God, Christian mission is incomplete. Proclamation must include word as well as example. These words may not be suitable for use with the non-Christian. However, some non-Christians may be intrigued by the depth of the vision when God is implied, even named. Remember that young adults, especially, are more likely to connect — or reconnect — with God-talk and church life through meeting Christians who are doing something caring or loving than through worship or Bible study.

7. How will I invite others to join me at Jesus' table to be fed and empowered to achieve this vision? (How will I encourage others to seek help in church life?)

Assumption: The Christian missionary must be part of a Christian congregation. The Word is read and spoken to clarify the purpose and direction of the mission. The Sacrament is shared to receive the power to carry on the mission.

(See Appendix A for these specific questions for each mission field and these and other hints for working with them.)

As I talked with the people whose stories follow, I began by asking, "What do you find yourself working on right now in that arena?" (This was a variation of the fourth question above.) I next asked, "What has been going on there that leads to you be working for that goal?" (This was the third question above.) We went on to talk a bit about what had happened so far. At that point, I usually said I would send along seven questions to reflect on and note their answers and to send them to me. Their responses were the starting point of our next phone call. I have found that variations of this approach help individuals and groups get started on the seven questions rather easily.

The stories that follow are told along the lines of these seven questions. You will probably be able to pick them out as you read each one. Each story begins with the specific mission. The fuller description of the missionary follows in the same way that getting to know our teammates occurs as we work with them over a period of time. ✦

Chapter 2 — At Home

Kit: A Mission of Quiet Time for a Working Mother

The number of working mothers continues to rise. Much of our future depends on their ability to provide wise and loving mothering. Kit takes up a regular quiet time to enhance the quality of life at home.

Courage to confront some issues

"God is giving me voice and courage to confront some issues. My faith that God is with me and loves me is growing. At a recent church conference, I was excited to discover that I could be loved and cared for without feeling dominated. I had avoided that feeling in both my spiritual and my personal living and shied away from some encounters. But, at the conference, none of the conference participants — male or female, clergy or lay — dominated the conversations. I talked with men — both clergy and lay — who were compassionate and supportive. It was a joy to be in a place where such equality was the norm.

For most of my life, I had felt dominated, especially by men. Feeling male dominated was the norm in my childhood at home and in my adult life. But, this isn't the case in my past or present church life.

I've joined a weekly art class. Conversations at the art class led me to suggest an oral Bible study (see p. 166) for interested class members, all women. I had learned this method at the conference and liked the way it helped to connect the Bible and daily life. During the Bible study, interest rose among some of the women to investigate women's issues in particular. So I set up a second group. We have been reading and discussing *She Who Is* by Elizabeth Johnson (Crossroad, 1994). The result of all this is growing in trust that God loves me as I am."

Too full, too fast, too electronic

"Home life has too much busy-ness. Life is too full, too fast, too electronic. There is too much love for material things. It all makes for too much pressure.

My husband, Larry, and our second grader, Heather, and I live in a rural area. I have two grown children by a previous marriage. I feel the load of working four out of five days a week — twenty-eight hours — and caring for a big house. I took the job as an accountant and bookkeeper because we needed the extra income. If it were up to me, I would work much less. Larry would like me to work more hours to better our lifestyle with, for example, a winter vacation.

When I look at my schedule, I don't know what I can give up. I take Heather to lessons and to extracurricular activities — swimming and skating and horseback riding. I would like to find piano and dance lessons for her. Long distances can make driving time for a lesson or an extracurricular activity take two hours. I find just keeping up with the laundry hard. Not all mothers do these things, but a lot of my friends do.

I need to adjust my priorities and live in a way that reflects internal values — call it practicing integrity. I need quiet, alone time. If I could give myself 15-20 minutes a day, it would help. I believe it would enhance everything. It is the refilling of my spirit. I can't pour out unless I am filled. I like, therefore, Joyce Rupp's *The Cup of Our Life: A Guide for Spiritual Growth* (Ave Maria, 1997), which uses the cup as a symbol for the inner journey. In it, she offers a method and readings for six weeks of daily meditation. These meditations refill one's cup of life. Contemplative, quiet time fills my cup and I can pour it out on Heather, her friends, and Larry."

Taking care of my own oxygen

"On an airplane, we are reminded to start our oxygen first, before we help the little ones. I need to take care of my own oxygen. I need to work toward making daily contemplative prayer a part of my life, as vital as breath. I need it to reach out to touch other lives. I need it to nourish my own soul. I can't share a journey that I don't walk. I have, at times, used the breath prayers for breathing in God's love and breathing out stress.

Therefore, I will work toward taking some quiet time each day. I can do it while driving to work by stopping along the road to pray or just taking a mindful walk and focusing on my breathing in and out while I walk. Reading and reflecting on the hymns also works for me. I want to quiet my mind. I might use contemplative prayer to empty my mind. I also like movement prayer, raising my hands, and praying to God. For me, this brings God down. I did this in the bathtub and a well of tears opened up! I will try to cook up something like this every day. I need to give myself time and space.

I will say, 'I need a period of time each day alone. Larry, Heather, please help me by just asking me if I have done it each day.' When I can, I will talk about how we all live in relationship with God and constantly strive for a closer relationship — even though we may not know it. I will talk of how we live in the light of God and reflect that light as we go about our daily lives. I will say, 'I hope all three of us can have a vision of living and sharing relationship with God.'"

An important part of my life

"'Often' is an operative word for me. I want to talk often about my journey with Heather and Larry and others in my family. I think daily remembrances are important — talking about God: 'God is good. God helps us. Thank you, God. I heard a sad story. God is here. God is with us. God helped with this problem. We need God's help with . . .'

I will encourage others by sharing and talking about what church means to me. I'll say things like:

'Let's go to church where we can talk to God and hear God's stories.'

'Church nourishes me by strengthening me, giving me hope, and renewing me to try to increase the number of times a week I take for quiet time.'

'It helps to know that if I fail, God still loves me.'

'It helps me to give myself for God to use.'

'For me, this is an important part of my life.'

Now, I talk like this a lot more than I used to."

Quiet time is like breakfast

While taking quiet time continues to be difficult, Kit now takes more time than she used to. On a recent vacation at the seashore, she found she could let the waves speak to her. She heard God saying to her to work on her physical health by walking and paying attention to her diet. "Take care of yourself, Lady," was the message she received. She calls it a familiar message that became urgent.

Once Kit returned home from a church conference to a family party the next day, then work on Monday, laundry, a birthday party for her daughter on Friday, and a guest family over the following weekend. The following Sunday brought her first free time when the others went hiking. First, she had to recall how to get into "her space." To help her, she used music and aromas and drew a bath.

Kit reads a lot of self-help books by women. She recalls a chapter from Anne Morrow Lindbergh's *Gift from the Sea* (Vintage, 1991) written during the sixties about how difficult it is for women to find solitude. In years past, Lindbergh writes, "Sunday worship was often the only time during the week women could be in their own soul."

Since seeking more quiet time, Kit tries harder to "stop and smell the roses." When frustrated and hurried, she tries harder to take moments to give a hug or kiss the top of Heather's head. These moments balance the chaos for her.

Kit met with support when she told her husband and daughter of her resolve to spend more time in reflection. She will ask her husband and daughter to inquire regularly if she is doing so. Since Larry questions some of the developments in their present congregation, Kit confines her comments about what church life might offer to how much it means to her.

Kit talks with Heather about God and quiet time as the core of things. "Quiet time is like breakfast. You need to do it in order to function," she says. She recently asked Heather what helps her to remember God's love. Heather replied, "Going to church a lot." More and more, Kit sees the results of Heather's participation in the church. Heather's comments reflect her sense of a daily walk with God. Often, when they meet someone in need, Kit and Heather offer two or three word prayers together.

Often, Heather and Kit pray for each other. In the middle of a meal, Kit coughed from choking. Heather prayed, "God, help her stop coughing and make her better." One night as they prayed together at bedtime, Kit kissed her and prayed for her, saying, "And I thank God for you, and for your vitality, and for your joy, and for your interest in so many things."

Kit meets with varying reactions from others beyond her family when she talks about how church life nourishes her. However, so far, none of the reactions have been negative. Some people react by showing their own interest in church and worship and go on to ask questions. Her baby-sitter recently asked, "What is worship like at your church?"

God in the here and now

After a period of inactivity, Kit resumed churchgoing with Larry as they began to go out together. When he went to church, she said simply, "I'd like to go with you." She had wanted to resume church life but, being alone, had not done so. Larry, himself, had been reawakened to church life during a cynical period when his secretary talked excitedly about her church and prayer life. C. S. Lewis' *Mere Christianity* (Macmillan, 1952) also helped him to get beyond his cynicism. During their engagement, the priest asked if they were ready to consider deeper commitment to the Christian way. Both reaffirmed their faith in confirmation. During the early years of their marriage, Kit still tended to go to church only when Larry was at home and not away on business.

Over the years, Kit found she stayed with the church because it renewed and sustained her through the week. She recalls a minister who said church was important "to help you be in relationship with God." For Kit that brought God down from an exalted patriarchal position to being with her in the here and now. The minister also said, "You do not come to church to be entertained." For Kit, that took churchgoing to "a different level."

God, relational and fair

Kit believes God is with us all the time giving us strength to discern what we need to do and how to do it. She comments, "Oral Bible study with its question about what is God calling me to do right now puts God in my life. God's presence in my everyday life is the basis of my spirituality." Kit found the warm support of the male clergy in her small group at the missionary spirituality conference a decisive moment. "God moved from being very patriarchal to be being very relational," as she puts it.

The basics of her faith are fairness and justice. This came from her parents. They worked hard for what they got and treated others fairly and equally. She saw her parents give equal gifts to both her sister and her sisters-in-law. When grandchildren came, each of them was treated equally. As she looks back, she has always lived her life around being fair. Now, she is more conscious that being fair is part of being a Christian. She tells of planning to give a plastic turtle sandbox Heather had outgrown to a poor child in need. A few days later, she heard that her grandson wanted it. She decided the fair decision was to give the sandbox to the child in need. Kit saw this moment as an early small step in becoming more aware of the Christian call to live justly. ✦

Jim: A Mission to Keep the Peace

Loving and wise fathering becomes harder and harder to provide as blended families, stresses on teens, and the difficulties of income maintenance increase. Jim lives out a mission to keep his home peaceful.

The father God wants me to be

"I need to raise my children to be Christian. I need to guide them along the way to love God and love their neighbor as themselves. I say to Teresa, my daughter by my first marriage, who is seventeen, 'Treat your brother better. Treat him the way you want to be treated.'

This has been a hard year. Teresa had a lot of rejection from her birth mother and it continues. She is receiving ongoing therapy to cope with it. I find her taking out her anger in arguments with Mary, my wife. Teresa also gets after the boys. She challenges Mary constantly and seems ready to pick a fight. This is very hard on Mary. Teresa, in particular, has special problems. I made some real mistakes in my first marriage when Teresa was little. Her mother did not want to spend time with her, so I agreed to let her leave the baby with her grandmother. As she grew up, Teresa feared birthdays because her mother said, 'You have only so many days until you are eighteen and I can kick you out of the house.' When Teresa's mother took up with another man, I asked her to leave. When Mary and I married, Teresa and Mary were getting along very well. In many ways, Mary doted on Teresa. Even after the births of the three boys, Mary continued to do as much as she could for Teresa.

My wife just lost her teaching job. She is slowly recovering from the disappointment and getting started on looking for a new job. Teresa's counselor believes Tommy, our five-year-old, transfers his anger at Teresa to Sam, our three-year-old. The boys get into arguments easily. Sam, though younger, seems to be a natural as an instigator to get Tommy into trouble. Luke, at eighteen months, is a joy.

I need to keep my own temper in the midst of arguments between family members, especially when I am part of an argument. I need to see that Teresa stays in her therapy. When I am at work, I need to be available by phone for Mary when things get too difficult.

I work at being a peacekeeper. I try to keep everyone from hurting each other. In particular, I try to spend more time with Teresa. And, I make sure that nothing interferes with her counseling. With all of them, I try to be consistent in discipline. I follow through with the consequences when they do not do what I've asked of them."

Keeping the peace

"Mary likes the idea of peacekeeping. But we have different styles of parenting. When it comes to discipline, I am harder on the boys than Mary is. Mary seems to have trouble making the boys leave her alone when she needs rest. I suspect they sense that they can get away with things with Mary. We keep talking about our different ways of raising them. We were thinking of placing Tommy and Sam in a Catholic school because we do not like the secular attitude of prekindergarten and public school.

I believe God has given me these children to guide and bring up right. To me that means helping them to love each other as good neighbors who live as close together as it is possible to live. When I discipline them, I try to do it out of concern for them rather than my anger. So, I pray for God's help to live this way with our children.

I try to put this approach into words with the children. I will say to Tommy, 'I am not happy with the way you are acting. God does not want you to act like this. God wants you to act toward your brother as you want him to act toward you. Don't complain that Sam hit you or took your toy when you just took his toy and hit him. Treat each other fairly, if you want to be treated fairly.'

With Teresa, I try to draw on her Happening experiences. [Happening is a weekend conference for tenth through twelfth graders that increases their spiritual formation as Christians. Its approach is both sacramental and evangelical. It develops a sense of individual commitment to Jesus Christ as Lord and Savior and of the eucharist as central to ongoing growth in and practice of the faith.] I will say to her, 'At Happening, you learn about the joys of God, and the closeness of God as being everywhere. Is this how you think you should be acting in God's eyes?' She will often blow it off with, 'Well, that doesn't count.'

For babies to receive communion was new to us, having come from the Catholic Church. Mary went to the annual convention of our neighboring diocese where the visiting bishop put the wafer directly into Tommy's one-year-old hand. Before Mary could say anything, he had eaten it. In time, we saw going to the communion rail come to be very special for him.

At a church conference, a clergy friend suggested we try 10-15 minutes of prayer together each day. We did for a little while but our schedules interfered. Mary actually prefers to pray by herself. Mary and I believe going to Jesus' table is belonging and getting his love and power inwardly. Now, we say to our children, 'You are going up there for something special. It is the body of Jesus, not just bread. You are taking some of church home with you. Jesus is telling you how much he loves you and wants you to spread that love.' We try to show it is all connected. We say, 'The man on the cross is Jesus. He died for us because he loves us.' I also talk with Teresa along these lines."

Calming down

"In the midst of a big argument with Mary two weeks ago, Teresa called me at work. I could tell from her voice that she was on the edge of doing something stupid. I calmed her down. When she is stressed, she has agreed to call her counselor or a church member who is a retired teacher. I tell Teresa that if what Mary asks is unreasonable, they need to talk it through. I tell her that, for the most part, she will have to do what is reasonably expected of her.

God has been helping me in the midst of these difficult weeks. One small way is Mary's two weeks of severance pay. And, the boys have been relatively calm. Putting them to bed has been easy enough. Even the dogs have been less difficult to manage!

About my being a peacekeeper, Mary says, 'Well, you can get them to listen at least.' Mary also calls me at work to resolve conflict with one of the boys. Sometimes I have to lay out what I will do, if one does not obey. And I follow up when I get home. So far, there is a relative peace at home — not as much as we would like but there is a peace there.

The boys read their 'God books' about Jonah and Noah and the like. They miss church when we are not able to go. Church starts with classes for them at 9:00 a.m. They come in at the Peace. Sam just enjoys going and knows church is special and does not want to be left out. He likes to 'get the Body of Jesus.' Tommy says he feels God's love. He is always up and chipper when he says, 'I feel God's love' or 'I feel God.' At home, if you forget their prayers at bedtime, they do not like it. Sam is not big on prayers, but Tommy loves the Lord's prayer. Mary has taught them to pray for sick friends — even for others to come over to play — and to give thanks when prayers are answered.

Teresa finished out her confirmation in the Catholic Church. Her mother and I were separated at the time and I had fallen away from church. However, I had promised her grandmother, during her last hours with us, to see that Terry was confirmed. Since then, the choir and Happening have come to mean a lot to Teresa. She has served on the staff of several Happenings. At her first staff, she was asked to talk on what has Jesus done for her. I helped her prepare using 1 Corinthians 13 and the theme of Jesus accepting you as you are. I got to read some of it, but she would not let me see it all. Teresa likes passing the bread and the cup from person to person at Happening. Now, church is more of a social event for Teresa. She does go up to receive freely. She is not as eager to talk about it as she used to be. When our priest asked about reaffirming her commitment and reception as an Episcopalian, she said she was not sure at this time.

Mary and I talk about how communion helps us. As I put it, 'Feeding on the body and blood of Jesus gives me more peace at heart.' Even though I have to work after church, I am more relaxed and peaceful. Overall, I feel more healed. The prayers after communion express a lot for me. After receiving, I use St. Francis' prayer too. I am looking for guidance and to be on stable ground. I find these prayers lead me in that direction. Mary uses the quiet time after communion to look at what she has done for the week and to feel more connected with Jesus' power for the week ahead."

Regular participants again

Jim and Mary have been married seven years. They are expecting another child in six months. Jim works nights as a planner and dispatcher for a trucking company, located about twenty minutes from their home. Mary is a qualified teacher and works intermittently.

Jim grew up in the Roman Catholic Church. As he encountered difficulties in his first marriage, Jim found the church's positions — compulsory presence at the Sunday mass and no divorce — blocked his wholehearted participation. He had lapsed almost completely until his relationship with Mary began to move toward marriage. Mary grew up in the Roman Catholic Church also. Once Mary was confirmed, her parents, believing they had done their job, only dropped her off at church and picked her up afterwards — often two hours or more later. By the end of college, Mary had dropped out as well. About ten months before their wedding, Jim and Mary began to visit many Roman Catholic churches.

Some of the sermon content, especially when it directed voting on the sole basis of a candidate's position on abortion, added to their reservations about the Catholic Church.

At the time, Mary was part of a college alumni choral group. The director, also an organist for an Episcopal church, invited her to church. She and Jim visited on Father's Day that year. The vitality of the minister in reading the Gospel and preaching, the warm and lengthy exchange of the Peace among all members of the congregation, and the gift of a rose to Jim as a father compelled them to visit again. After several Sundays, they began premarital instruction. They have been regular participants in Episcopal congregations ever since.

God, both fair and caring

Describing his faith, Jim says, "I believe in Jesus as our Savior and that I need to work to be more Christlike in my actions and speech. I believe I need to love God and my neighbor as myself. I try not to degrade others. If I get mad at someone, I try not to curse at them. I try to be as calm as possible in a hot situation. When I have conflict with one of my supervisors, I try not to say anything. I try to pull him aside and ask, 'What is the problem? What have I done to irritate you?'

I believe God is very fair. For every action there is a reaction. If you are constantly doing wrong, you might get away with it for your whole life with good health and wealth but eventually you will go to God and you will pay. You will find out, Yes, you should have been more kind. I learned God is fair from my religion teachers in my Catholic high school. One teacher, a priest, had been a very successful stockbroker making lots of money. At the school, he formed Children of Glory, a retreat group. One weekend, five or six high schoolers came to disrupt things. By the end of the first night, they were more into it than the rest of us. He brought in popular songs and would ask, 'What is this saying to you? What is God saying to you?' He also brought in fairness when we playacted the Gospel for the week. He was the first priest I had met in sixteen years who knew what the real world was like.

I believe that God takes care of everything. There have been times when we had no money and I opened the mailbox to find an insurance rebate. Another time, a class action suit I had forgotten about resulted in a check coming in a time of need. I see these events as signs of God looking out for us. He is there helping. He does not make it easy. He does not give everything to you. You have to work for it. He does provide when you need it. He will not let you fall flat on your face. He is there to help you and to pick you up. A billboard says, 'Trouble? Try prayer.' I believe in that."

Describing his ethics, Jim says, "Not to degrade others and to watch your temper are the biggest for me. In my late twenties, I learned this from observing other people. I had moved out of home when I was seventeen. At twenty, I was married with my first child. I worked in food service, in trucking, and for UPS. I saw people living without degrading others, keeping their temper, and life seemed to work better for them. As I started getting back into my faith in the Episcopal Church, I came to see I wanted to be more Christlike. There had been a lot of discord in my first marriage. I began to ask how I wanted to live and I found answers in my faith. I draw on the Lord's Prayer — be forgiven and forgive. Love the Lord your God and your neighbor. I like 1 Corinthians 13 — 'love is not boastful.' I like St. Francis' prayer — 'Where there is hatred, let us sow love.' I help someone in need knowing that, one day, someone will help me out. Now, people come to me, expecting they will not be yelled at. They don't have to hide a mistake. They don't seem to fear asking me a question." ✦

Leila: A Mission of Learning to Form a Good Child and Citizen

At home mothers must cope with a maze of choices in child guidance and the high mobility that separates mothers from the help of other caregivers. After a fulfilling work experience, Leila chooses to learn about staying home to mother her child.

Things to do and to change

"Home is where I belong right now in my life. Since my working years were fulfilling, I do not feel the loss of self that many new mothers feel. And, I believe, mothering will fill in some holes in my experience and leave me better prepared for my future missions in life.

Right now, I resent it that Don gets to 'escape' the dailiness of home life. Boredom and lack of intellectual stimulation can make the daily tasks of teaching and forming a child daunting and thankless.

I need to get out alone to recharge my batteries. I need time alone with Don to keep our relationship on track. I need more prayer to deal with

Tommy and all that comes my way. I am always learning about parenting. Books and conversations with other parents help to alert me to the inner workings of family life. As I understand more, I do better. Understanding the context helps me to be a just parent. But I will be fooled from time to time. I will hear about a parenting approach, try it, and hate it. But God calls me back. The things I try can, somehow, leave me feeling I am doing the wrong thing. So I pray and talk to other parents whom I respect. Then, I am, eventually, led to the right approach. Once I make it my own, things with my child begin to click as, I believe, God wants them to.

I have to be clear with Don about my need for time off from mothering. I have to be sure not to react in anger too much with Tommy. I need to act with forethought about what the outcome is that I want to achieve. This will help me to form a good child and citizen.

I will try to give Tommy a reality-based reason whenever I say 'no' — a reason that he can understand. I came across an example in my reading recently. When Tommy grabs things off the rack at the checkout line, I will try to say more than, 'Don't do that.' I will try to tell him why he should not do that. I will try to say, 'Someone worked hard to get those hung up there. They will have to do extra work just to put them back if you pull them down.'

I will express my need for time off in ways that show a recognition of Don's need for time off as well. 'How about you fly on Sunday, Don, and, Saturday afternoon, I'll go see my friend?'

I will work to remember first that God wants Don and me to have a super marriage and wants us to be excellent parents. I will pray, 'God, help me to get there. This is my goal, too.' I will go to church with Don and get involved with people. I will see that my God-talk is about the positive things that God is doing and wants for us all.

I will try to suggest to people that they go to church because it can improve the quality of their lives. I will remind them that church can give their kids a solid foundation, regardless of what happens in their lives. I will share with others, 'I go to church because my week always goes better after a Sunday service. I've found that the more often I go, the better other things get. That's why I try to go every Sunday.'"

Raising a good person

Leila says that Don has responded well to her requests for time alone. He likes the "trades" as she calls them. He gets time to fly and she gets time out with her friends. She also says that people in her Moms' group have reacted with respect and general acceptance to her talk of God and the church. While two of the group have gone to church, Leila is cautious in claiming just how much her words influenced them. She is glad that she found a way to share her convictions with them.

Leila has discovered a book about discipline that really excites her: *Shepherding a Child's Heart* by Tedd Tripp (Shepherd Press, 1995). She had found most books presented discipline as the way to get control of your child; to make your life easier; or to make your child more cooperative. While she has reservations about some sections, she likes the way this book presents the primary objective of discipline as making a good person. Moreover, it presents this goal in the framework of Christian faith. The key is constantly communicating your values. The vision of raising a good person as the parents' mission at home excites her to the point of wanting to start another mothers' group centering on this view of discipline.

Help for the tough times

Leila had been married six years when she became pregnant. After reaching the rank of captain as a company commander in the Army, she returned to civilian life as a computer expert and secured a master's degree in business. At that point, she decided to stay home with her newborn, who is now almost two years old. She and her husband expect a second child in a few months.

Leila has been a sporadic participant in Episcopal worship throughout her life. During her childhood, the family went to church every Sunday. As she puts it, "That was it." During her college years, she worshiped only a handful of times. After college, she went into the Army. Life was tough for her there and she worshiped more frequently. "I needed help anywhere I could get it and I found life was better when I went to church." In marriage, her husband cooperates with her desire to seek out Episcopal congregations.

Leila learned her ethics and values at home. She built on them with other experiences. In the sixth grade, she saw a movie on the harmful results of drug use. It was so graphic she resolved never to become addicted. During adolescence, she never went along with her friends who were commending the use of drugs and sex. She tried beer and marijuana "a couple of times" and avoided having a sexual experience altogether. Leila is keenly aware of issues around women, race, poverty, and the environment. ✦

Wayne: A Mission to Cope with One's Defensiveness

Retirement offers chances for deepening a marital relationship that requires continued growth in emotional maturity. Wayne discovers coping with his defensiveness is essential for his marriage to continue to blossom.

Retirement riches

"Betty and I were married in 1954. We have been on a third honeymoon since my retirement in 1993. We are blessed with a degree of joy and intimacy, in all its aspects, that I never expected or even imagined! I've never heard anyone say that marriages might have their greatest chance to blossom late in the marriage. And, like young couples, we find we are still getting to know each other. That is the way I've been led to see the disagreements that arise between us. We have never been together this much before. We forget that we are still getting to know each other.

I find I still need to grow as a person. In times of disagreement, I can become defensive and feel wounded. I need to remember that we are getting to know each other better and to recognize that there is yet one more difference to resolve. From my side, I need to speak up, rather than swallow my sense of being attacked. Next, I need to listen with care to my wife's response. I need to be ready to discern from her response whether or not my defensiveness is the real problem.

I need to be aware of my tendency to take offense. I will seek to talk it out — even if we get noisy! Then, put it behind me and move on! I'll say, 'Let's keep working things out. At times, I see I'm just taking offense. Other times, I realize that we just do things differently and, so, we're learning a little more about each other.'

I find I often refer to the vision of working through my defensiveness indirectly during our daily Bible study. We try to read half a chapter of a Gospel and then each talks about 'what do I hear God calling me to do today.' Then we each pray for the other to be able to do it. Almost always there is an implication for our life together. It's fun to joke about it as we acknowledge the implication. One day her prayer was to speak out against evil. I prayed, 'Help Betty to speak out against evil — but go easy if it's in me.'

I look for times to tell people that, yes, there is lots of stress in being on mission with each other, our kids and their families, the church, the local community, and the wider world. I find help to bear the stress in the bread and the cup of communion. There I am fed with power to avoid taking things personally — even more, to hang in with all the missions I believe I am called to.

I recently found myself saying to Betty, 'I think I am going to let you be yourself from now on!' Fortunately, she understood my left-handed humor to hear the fulfilment I was finding and continue to find."

Timely answers

"Today's premium on authenticity calls for a story of my own! We have been married for forty-six years and have lived in a comfortable home overlooking Lake Champlain in Essex, New York for the past seven years. Our two sons and two daughters are married. We take grandparenting seriously with twelve grandchildren — five came with the second marriage of one of our sons — in the four families spread from Saratoga Springs in New York to Germany. Betty and I are deeply involved in our local congregation. She is, at present, a warden and I am a volunteer assisting priest. Betty continues to paint and frame in a well-equipped shop out back. I carry on this Missionary Spirituality project, participate in local school affairs, co-chair a senior housing project, serve on the town and county Democratic committees, and sail as often as I can.

I have always been an Episcopalian. Sunday worship began at age six with my parents. We were part of early morning communion so my father could get to his real estate work by 10:00 a.m. I began to ask questions about Christianity, in general, and ordained ministry and church leadership, in particular, in my early teens. I was blessed with a minister who could answer my questions in ways that both satisfied me and encouraged further inquiry. Inquiry and helpful responses from clergy continued through college.

I went to seminary to concentrate on my religious quest as the way to decide about ordination. Seminary provided abiding answers to my questions, especially how reason depends on faith, how God is met through people, and how God calls us to be just as well as to be loving. During the first year in seminary, my daily pattern of meditation and prayer began to take shape; during that first year, a central moment came when a professor provided this insight — that the Christian did not live to get home but started out from home. Since I had never really felt 'at home,' this insight proved decisive. When I walked out of the building that morning, I had a vision of Jesus. That sense of personal encounter moved me toward ordination. Subsequent reading, refresher courses, Cursillo (see p. 33), Marriage Encounter (see p. 83), and spiritual formation have added valuable dimensions to my journey."

Learnings in ethics

"Training in ethics began in seminary. I understand love and justice and the imperfection of all things human as the heart of Christian ethics. I began to learn how to apply these basics the year following seminary. The seminary had recommended a delay of ordination, since I had gone straight from high school to college to seminary. The next year, I learned something of the ethics of marketing while selling Fuller Brush products. I was ordained in 1954. More learnings in ethics were shaped by experiences in Christian education development; training in leadership of both small groups and systems; work for civil rights and community organizations; in-depth encounter with the lay academies of Europe in the sixties and seventies; and further training as a counselor. Serving on the national church staff gave me some invaluable encounters with the people of developing nations. Finally, I learned much about church leadership and mission working with James D. Anderson, an independent consultant to all levels of church life." ✦

Chapter 3 — At Work

Margaret: A Mission to Resolve Tension with a Co-worker

Maintaining wholesome relationships with one's co-workers is central to productive daily work. Margaret works through a difficult relationship at work.

A tough assignment

"I think God has been calling me to Christianize my work environment, almost from the moment I got there. In general, I work out of a belief in abundance. Fear of scarcity forgets that God provides what we really need at all times. You can share without fear of losing your own position or self-confidence or faith. Therefore, I do not fear for my job. I give myself to it doing the best I can and maintaining collegial and caring relationships with the other workers — supervisors, peers, and those I supervise. I also try to work this way with our clients.

I am struggling in a relationship with a co-worker. A new person, Esther, has taken a job I turned down. The job would have paid more, but it would have interfered with my parenting. Esther is just out of college. It is my job to train her. She seems extremely ambitious and ready to advance at my expense. When her supervisor criticizes something both of us have worked on, she blames me for the error, saying, 'That was Margaret's job. I don't know why those numbers were not checked.' Further, when praised for work both of us have done together, she takes full credit for it. She could have cost me my job. There are times I have to sit on my anger and be content to pray, 'God, you have to love that person for me because I can't right now.'

I need to pray for guidance in my relationship with Esther. I need to trust God and to let go of the sense that I would lose something by helping her — even if it means losing my own job. I will recall my sense of abundance and let go, and give myself to training Esther, even overtraining her so she can do the job well. I will find a time to reassure Esther that she has nothing to fear from me and that her success will be success for me too. I will talk with Esther along the lines that she need not fear me and that I want her to succeed. If she does well and is happier, I will be happier, too.

I will let my trust in God's provision for us both flavor my talk with her in whatever way is natural at the time. I love the congregation I am part of so I am always encouraging people to visit it. I will probably find occasion to invite Esther."

No longer a threat

Margaret found a time to sit down next to Esther. She said, "Esther, you need to stop being afraid of me." Esther responded, "I am not afraid of you." Margaret commented, "You are, if you feel you have to lie to people about me. I am not a threat to you. I want you to succeed. If you succeed, you will be happy and, if you are happy, then my workplace is happy. I have no reason not to support you in doing everything you need to do. I am secure in who I am. I will not take anything from you. God provides for us all." At first, Esther seemed shocked but then relaxed a bit saying, "I'm not sure what you are talking about." Margaret repeated what she said and Esther relaxed more.

Margaret still has difficult times with Esther. At times, Margaret has to cut their conversation short and go to her cubicle to pray to let go and "to see Christ in Esther."

As time passed, Esther let her guard down a great deal. Now, Esther comes to Margaret's cubicle when she is in a stressful personal situation. Esther is a single mother, as is Margaret, and has problems dealing with her former husband and her daughter. Margaret sees her already beginning to shape her life around Christian values. Esther has had a hard life and is just now beginning to soften up. Esther marvels at how Margaret makes ends meet, since Margaret makes less than Esther does. Margaret keeps saying, "God provides."

About six months after the frank talk about their relationship, an occasion arose when Margaret invited Esther to church. Another woman in the office was planning to visit Margaret's church. Since Esther was standing there at the time, it was natural for Margaret to suggest Esther come along. After church, they would have lunch and pick peaches. Esther declined saying she saw church as taking away from her time with her daughter. Margaret replied, "Do come whenever you want to." Margaret notes that

Esther has talked of bad experiences in fundamentalist Protestant church-es and may have fear of things religious.

After another six months, Esther surprised Margaret during a work break. Esther came into the break room as Margaret was talking. Margaret mentioned an incident from the children's videotape series, "Veggietales," which is scripture retold with animation. Esther's face lit up. She had pur-chased the video for her daughter. It seems that Esther's gym is owned by Christians who talked to Esther about their Pentecostal church. They had suggested the videotape series when Esther seemed interested in some kind of Christian formation for her daughter. Esther commented that she was planning to visit the church with them soon. Margaret saw this as what she calls "a modern day miracle."

Crystals to prayer

At this time, Margaret reports a high turnover of employees. She finds the new workers are either Christians wearing pectoral crosses or "Christian-curious" as she puts it. The Christians comment on the cross or the Bible in her cubicle and say things like, "That's a beautiful cross — I have one too," or "Oh, are you a Christian? I am too."

One of the Christian-curious asked to borrow a Bible several months ago. When Margaret brought it in, the inquirer asked to be shown how to read it and what the books meant. Margaret answered and encouraged her to keep the Bible as long as she needed it. As time passed, her co-worker occasionally questioned Margaret further. Each time, Margaret concluded her answers with an invitation to visit her church. She reassured her that the dress was casual and that she would sit with her to help her partici-pate. Eventually, the co-worker said yes. Margaret learned this would be the first time that her co-worker, a young adult, had ever been to a church. The co-worker has a blended family. She is now expecting the first baby with her husband. The Sunday she and her husband went with Margaret, her husband was touched deeply by the method used for confession. Each person held a stone and recalled silently his or her confession. Then, each person took the stone to the table where the pastor washed it in water. After the liturgy, the husband remarked how that confessional experience had relieved his conscience with a sense of the Spirit washing over him. Hearing they were moving more than a thousand miles to a new home that week, Margaret asked the priest to lay hands on the mother-to-be for a safe trip for all. The co-worker is seeking an Episcopal church near their new home.

Another person, Lisa, came to the department full of new age ideas and talk of crystals. One day, she joined Margaret's coffee break sharing with two others with whom Lisa talks often. Lisa asked, "Don't you think God is an overwhelming positive force." Margaret answered, "No, God is my father." "What do you mean?" Lisa asked. Margaret said, "God created me. He is where I come from and where I am going." Lisa said, "Don't you think Jesus was just a highly advanced person — a psychic or something." Margaret returned, "He certainly possessed gifts of the Spirit. But Jesus died for my sins. He was God made flesh." They talked more. Margaret has noticed that Lisa has stopped "new age talk" and now says, "I think I need to pray." When Lisa received a bonus for some good work, she said, "I have to thank God for this." Lisa continues to question and to listen. Recently, Lisa was made Margaret's personal assistant.

Margaret finds about eight openly Christian people on her floor; they receive prayer requests and exchange gestures of friendship and mutual support. In times of stress, she and two other people in her section often meet during the regular coffee break for prayer.

Okay to go back

Margaret is an administrative assistant for two vice-presidents of an environmental cleanup firm. She is responsible for contract compliance for her company and supervises two people. She is a single mother with three children at home, an eleven-year-old boy and twin girls who are nine years old.

Margaret came back to church as a member of the walking wounded, newly divorced from a nine-year marriage where there had been domestic violence. "To be specific, my husband used to hit me for crying because he hit me. I learned to move into a really contemplative state in my mind and start talking to God. I prayed, 'Please let us fall asleep. Please let us be safe. Please let it be ended.' Then I would get quiet. Then I would listen. Then I would get small bits of comfort. As a child, I was taught to pray as I went to bed so I was in the habit of praying every night of my life.

I simply needed a place to belong. It was my background in the Episcopal Church that helped me to return. The church had pulled me through the darkest times in my life. I now have nine years as a recovered alcoholic. I was still using alcohol when I married. When I was completely isolated from the church, the only place my former husband would let me go alone was to the church. He was an atheist. His controlling nature led him to follow me to the church so that he could know what I was doing. Probably to his own surprise as much as to my own, he came to ask to be baptized. After a coed Cursillo [a three-day and three-night spiritual formation weekend for adults available in many Episcopal dioceses and the judicatories of many other communions], he decided to be confirmed. Although he never could quite tame the spirit that drove him into his rages, I can let go and forgive him. I can trust God's work with him and I do not have to be a victim of his rages anymore."

Margaret found her present congregation in the midst of a time of being overwhelmed with guilt over her divorce. There was an event one night that changed her. "I felt I had failed as a Christian wife. I finally collapsed under the pressure. We were in a safe apartment with the three kids safely tucked in bed. It was late at night. I was on my knees bawling as the overwhelming pain got me. I was begging God to forgive me. I felt a presence near me. Out of the corner of my eye, I saw a light and I knew it to be my Lord Christ. I felt a hand on my shoulder and this overwhelming peace flowed through me. I turned and looked and Jesus was laughing. And this voice in my head said, 'It's okay. It's what I expected you to do.' And it was gone. In passing, I heard, 'Open the phone book.' I opened it and there was the name of the church and an ad saying 'An Episcopal Church demonstrating God's unconditional love.' I had to drive forty-five minutes from our dingy apartment to the church. I left church that Sunday feeling it was okay to go back. My loneliness and my hunger to belong took me back the next Sunday. I have made the trip ever since. God put me there. The love I felt from the minister and the community she led was so prevalent, so inviting that I just stayed. I signed up for a few things here and there, but after a particularly moving and poignant Ash Wednesday, I found myself called to forgiveness. I had found forgiveness for myself and, now, I forgave my former husband. I could not go back into the grief, into the darkness, into being away from the church, into being away from God."

Finding out the hard way

Margaret's faith was shaped by the Episcopal Church, where she was born and raised, and is centered in God and daily practice. She says, "I completely and totally believe that, if it were not for the living and dying of my Savior, Jesus, I would be so paralyzed with fear, guilt, and doubt that I would be unable to go on doing the good work of my Father in heaven. I acquired this faith both from being steeped in the lessons of the church and from rebelling, rejecting the lessons, and finding out the 'hard way' that God was right all along. It was in that hard, dark place, where I had nothing to depend on but my faith, that I learned how to bring God into the hell I was living.

I discovered I was not really ever alone. I could always pray. So, in those dark places when all I could do was pray, I prayed. Daily prayer became as much a part of my survival-skill package as coping with the co-dependency that surrounds abusive marriages, and as 12-step meetings for an alcoholic.

Both of my parents were very devout. I have a brother three years younger than I. I was raised in an extremely spirit-filled household. It was not unusual to stop in the middle of the day for a prayer of thanksgiving or for help. My parents made their Cursillo in 1967. I was making *palanca* [from the Spanish meaning 'lever' and used for a 'lever' of prayer for a participant to turn to Jesus Christ as Lord and Savior; it has come to be applied to anything from letters to banners made by former participants to support and encourage a Cursillo weekend — in this case, hand-decorated place mats] for Cursillos before I could say the word. I am active in Cursillo myself, today. While both of my parents were alcoholics, they were not neglectful or abusive. They were loving, generous people and still are. Two to three drinks a night was not uncommon. It was their way to relax.

In that atmosphere, I began to drink actively when I was ten. I was twenty-one the first time I got sober. I struggled for three more years and I was twenty-four before I figured out how to do it. I was married at twenty-two and had three kids. I was sober during pregnancy but the celebratory glass of champagne after giving birth got me started again. Someone gave me a big book about Alcoholics Anonymous. As I read it, I found I was reading my own life. I started crying. I shut the book, put it away, and ignored it. The church I went to at that time had a 12-step program for overeaters. I felt that was sort of like AA and would go there to lose weight. I cross-addicted a lot. I had a food addiction and used food a lot. I weighed 385 pounds at one point. Since I was pretty convinced I would kill myself, I went to that group. As I got into it, I came to see my real disease was not the food, but the alcohol. I went to work on the problem, then."

Margaret summarizes her ethics this way: "My ethics are based on the two great commandments Jesus gave — 'to love God with all my heart, soul, strength, and mind;' and 'to love my neighbor as myself.' I acquired these ethics from the church and from scripture. I learned how to apply them (and am still learning as it is a daily cross) from the community of God.

I learned most about how to apply my ethics in daily life from the 12-step programs. I read scripture a lot. If I have a question, I find my answer somewhere in the Bible. I don't always like the answer. Obedience has never been my strong point. As for the problem passages, I pray for a discerning heart, ability to see what He wants me to do, and the ability to interpret His word. I am not a literalist. I use commentaries. I like Chuck (Charles R.) Swindoll and C. S. Lewis and Max Lucado. When I need more help, I call our pastor." ✦

George: A Mission to Speak Up

It takes a blend of tact and courage for workers to differ with their supervisors. George, a letter-carrier, discerns the need to speak up about work conditions and does so.

Wanted: a more joyful place

"I knew I was called to be more compassionate and understanding. There was more than a paycheck involved here. There was a lot of division and a lot of misunderstanding because people were afraid to address the issues that concerned them.

There was a fear of speaking out and, as a result, animosity between the union, management, and workers. We talked of each other in categories as if we were automatons. 'All managers are liars and cheats.' 'The union is just a propaganda machine.' 'The workers are overpaid and lazy to boot.'

Openness and communication were needed. All of us were seeking some form of justice. We needed more workers. We had too much work and not enough people. We all needed to realize that all of us wanted to be happy in our work. I wanted to see a more joyful place.

I decided I would get to know how people were feeling and open up the issues in our weekly service talks. That was where I could level and bring things out before the whole office. I did not want to humiliate a supervisor, but to get an issue out where people felt a bit freer to talk about it. Service talks were expected to be a place where we could dump off our gripes.

I decided I would try to be open to all the ideas and opinions. I would try to find common ground.

And, I decided I would pray to be of more use around there. I would be more alert to where I could help. My congregation's sessions on mission in our daily lives had made me more aware of lost opportunities."

George describes the weekly service talks as gatherings around the supervisor's desk, saying: "Sometimes it is a safety talk such as how to be safe in hot weather. Sometimes it is about a new program. Sometimes it is the head office wanting something done better. Often, it ends up in a question and answer session. It increases awareness by the workers of what is going on and the workers come to see that they are not alone in what they think. It may bring about some action on management's part. Most often the action taken was a Band-Aid".

Each of us a human being

"I believed it would be a wonderful thing for us to recognize each other as human beings worthy of respect and dignity, instead of as categorized automatons. When talking with a co-worker about the supervisor's temperament, I would say things like, 'She has her problems and stresses too. She wants to find some happiness in her life, just like the rest of us.'

I don't feel free to be very direct with religious talk. My childhood in an Assembly of God church had made me think I should but I don't feel free to do so. Everyone does know I am part of a church and that church means a lot to me. So, in these service meetings, I would have to imply a wider reference saying something like, 'In order to be happier and more fulfilled in our work, we need to have open dialogue. All of us have gifts and basic human dignity. We must treat all sides fairly, expressing compassion and concern on a level deeper than our disagreements.'

I believe God is present in every situation. How I might talk of God would come as a surprise — mostly to me! I could not plan how God would choose to lead me, but I could try to be open to God's leading and prepared to follow when that time came.

So far, I have been able to speak up and give voice to concerns that are common to the workers because I see God as a greater authority than the people who pay us. My desire for reconciliation at the Post Office has coincided with an increased involvement in church life of which I talk often. It gives me joy and strength. There is a visible connection and, I hope, something others see as a means to help them also.

Communication, honesty, and understanding come from my involvement in church life and sharing in the body of Christ, who wants us all to be empowered and fed by His love for us. When I am asked 'How do you do it, George?' and 'What keeps you going?' I reply, 'I'm involved in things outside of work that keep me going. My involvement in my church helps a lot. It could help you too.'"

Suddenly my mouth was open

George started speaking up about a year after he came back to church. He was very frustrated with the new supervisor at work at that time. The supervisor had been brought in to "straighten out the branch" — as George puts it. This got George's "dander up." He reports, "I had imagined myself speaking up but had not yet done so. Then, all of a sudden, my mouth was open. Somehow, I had found the courage and was speaking up."

The occasion was a service meeting where the supervisor was complaining about a rumor going around the branch. The rumor portrayed the supervisor as manipulating the day's workload so that a specific carrier completed her route early and he would have a reason to justify adding to her route. The supervisor complained to the workers that it was not true, and, if continued, could get back to the main office and cost him his job. George had not heard the rumor. To counter the supervisor's accusatory manner, George said, "I'm sorry, but I didn't hear anything about this and I feel kind of left out. I don't know anything about this rumor." The supervisor thought George was being facetious and was trying to humiliate him in front of the others. George, himself, was fed up and tense. He left the meeting for a break. The meeting broke up soon after he left. Later, George learned that a number of people had not heard of this "rumor" either. It seemed the supervisor, new to the office, was asserting his power. His concern was valid, but instead of making an effort to clear the air, he made a broad accusation against all the workers.

After the meeting, the supervisor drew George aside and said, "Don't you ever upstage me in front of the whole office again. I really don't appreciate it." George responded, "Well, if there is a rumor going around, it needs to be talked about. Would you rather it stay under the surface and fester or would you rather talk about it out in the open with everybody?" The supervisor repeated, "Well, you shouldn't upstage me in front of everybody," and walked away.

George began to encourage his co-workers to speak up. While there was some initial hesitation and resistance, the overall result has been positive. They began to seek him out saying, "That's really what I was thinking — that he was being unfair — and I am glad you found a way to stop it." Lest he go too far at some time, George has begun to consult with one or two people about speaking up. So far, he has been told, "That's on our minds too. Go for it."

A recent occasion concerned the submission of inflated figures for work performance being sent to the main office. The main office concluded that the branch was doing fine work and did not need any extra personnel. The union steward found out about the inflated figures, investigated, and learned they were due to omitting the hours of a worker who was setting up routes and putting the mail in order for carriers. The omission was corrected. Later, the steward mentioned the incident to six or seven of the workers, including George. When they heard about it, George and the others were disappointed they had no airing of it with management. Since they were being overworked, this was a serious omission to them. At a service meeting, George brought up the matter. His doing so has led to the discussion of adding a regular worker to meetings of the union and management to provide a forum to express the thoughts and feelings of the workers so that they will not be left to fester.

George's speaking up has been an icebreaker. Workers saw that George was not attacked for speaking up. They now feel more at ease just talking among themselves about these kinds of concerns. They have been assured they will not be harassed or have their days off canceled because management finds out they have been talking.

George has also talked with the supervisor about bringing up more positive things at the service and production talks. At the service talks, often, only one positive thing is named followed by fifteen minutes of things management sees as wrong. These faults range from not producing enough to summertime shorts not being the right length, working with sleeves rolled up, and socks not pulled up to the specified height. George observes that management forgets what it is like "to have a bag on your back."

The union seems to forget too. The union is more concerned with holding up the terms of the contract. In the back and forth between union and management, the workers get lost. An undertow of negative feelings and unresolved personal issues builds. These frustrations really make a difference when the heavy load of holiday mail comes around at Christmas.

Accordingly, George has told the supervisor these feelings are as important as the contract. George reports the present supervisor respects him for speaking up and voicing the feelings others may be afraid to talk about. George does not fear losing his job. He knows that he does his job and that he selects his battles with care.

Indirect God-talk

While most of his references to God are indirect, George senses these references are grasped by others. They know how meaningful the church is to him and, on occasion, turn to him about it. A co-worker came to him sharing that his wife wanted baptism but was not sure where to seek it. The couple had been in classes for baptism but became skeptical when the church sent them a bill for the child care it provided during the classes. George consulted his pastor, who suggested the co-worker think of baptism as acceptance into a family and, therefore, find a church family he and his wife wanted to be part of and talk with them about baptism. The co-worker followed the advice and he and his family are now part of a Baptist church.

When George hears about people facing a crisis, he prays for them and asks his congregation to pray for them. One man's wife was anxious about having a hysterectomy. When she came through it safely, the husband said with gratitude and wonder, "I don't know how you people pray at that church, but my wife really did well and I want to thank you."

George seeks times to talk of God to others without being pushy about it. Once a worker was having a hard day with too much to do and the prospect of overtime. The worker said, "What I really need is for the calvary to come riding in." George joked, "Calvary might be just the thing you need." The worker, very reticent about religion, responded quickly, "No, no, I mean cavalry." Since then, his colleague often greets him with, "Well, what's the word today, Georgie?" When he replies, for example, "Compassion — I need more compassion," his colleague will switch the subject quickly. George surmises, "I know he is seeking but he does not want to be verbal about it. He knows where I am coming from. I don't want to beat him over the head because I have been in that position and didn't like it."

Quitting the job to work for God

George and his wife have a son, sixteen, and two daughters, eight and seven. As noted, George grew up in an Assembly of God congregation.

Some difficult experiences with members of the congregation were part of the beginning of his lapse from participation at sixteen. College lacked purpose for him and he left to go to work. After a number of different jobs, he went to work for the post office at twenty.

Three years ago, George was despairing over his employment. He seriously considered quitting his job to move to a place where he could make ends meet on a smaller income. While weighing such a move, he sensed that God was telling him to stay where he was because exciting things were going to happen. George came to feel that he should go back to church and that church participation would become an integral part of his life. He had not worshiped in a church in four years.

He was living near the place where he had grown up. Across the street was St. Francis Episcopal Church. One day he was praying about his work as he turned into his driveway. He glimpsed the church across the street and sensed it might have something for him. He was partial to the name "Francis" because a close friend had been become a Franciscan and George had "hung out" with him and the Franciscans at a Roman Catholic church for a time. He also remembered a crossing guard from his childhood. She belonged to St. Francis and he was sure he would find her there now. As he began to worship there, he heard they had no music at the 8:00 a.m. liturgy. He offered to play the guitar for them. The congregation loved it and he has been playing ever since.

George came to share his frustrations at work with the pastor in the course of their frequent conversations. At about this time, the priest decided to call together a group to experiment with the seven questions (pp. 10 and 11) for discerning mission in life's daily arenas. Remembering George was having a hard time, the pastor suggested he join the weekly sessions. George would often come to the sessions thinking he had nothing to talk about or to offer. Invariably, he found he had things to say and to offer and that participating in the sessions was, as he put it, "a good thing."

George continued his prayers about his work; he was fed up and wanted out. But, financially, he saw he had no other alternative. One time he reflected, "You are talking to the Creator. That counts for something that is more powerful than a paycheck." He reflected further, "Whether I am there or not, God is the final authority. I have nothing to fear from that place. There is a security that employment and benefits cannot offer." Next, George found himself asking God if he should go to work in the morning. He would pray for the people there as he walked the four blocks to work. As he later put it, "I quit my job to go to work for God."

Teens search together

George summarizes his faith as "subverting the dominant paradigm." The radical nature of the faith appeals to him. He thinks of the little person being stepped on and then being able to stand up and say what is true and what one is deeply convinced about. This kind of experience is what really "sticks out of Christianity" for him. Jesus' confrontation with the money changers in the Temple (Mark 11:15-19) and with the Pharisees about tribute to Caesar (Mark 12:13-17) and whose picture is on the coin are typical of the person with little power taking on the dominant.

This approach to Christian faith was picked in his exchanges with his friends during middle and late adolescence. They were struggling together to find their way with the church and with the rest of their lives. His friend, who was contemplating becoming a Franciscan, lent a special reality to their mutual struggle.

George learned the value of honesty and truth from his mother. Not going along with the crowd is another basic for him. Not conforming to the world came from both his fundamentalist church and his mother. Learning to live this way came from what he calls the "hardheadedness of adolescence" as he coped with the hypocrisy of his parents alongside how wonderful they were. He tried to show how much truer he was to the ideals of truth, honesty, and nonconformity to the world than they were. The result was to "propel him," as he puts it, in the direction of making these principles his own for life. ✦

Eddie: A Mission to Analyze What Goes Wrong at the Law Office

Like everyone else, professionals need supportive relationships to work effectively. Eddie, a lawyer, leads his legal team to analyze what goes wrong, rather than to blame a team member.

To avoid anxiety

Eddie manages a practice group in his law firm. A practice group is a team that has a marketing and/or a particular focus for its legal practice, such as information technology or estate planning. There are seventeen partners and five associate lawyers within the group. Eddie is responsible for coordinating their generation of business, collections, training, and expenses.

"When a case or transaction does not go right for a client, there is much pain and resentment aroused in those responsible. Life is a wonderful gift but it is hard and was never meant to be easy. You use the Gospel as your source of hope and you strive forward trying to do your best to live up to its precepts, recognizing you have feet of clay and are bound to fail. There is a clear infusion in my thinking of the Ten Commandments. And there are Christ's declarations to his disciples and to others: 'Love one another;' 'Put others before yourself;' and 'Turn the other cheek.'

When something does not go right, my typical response is, 'Well, we have got to figure out what we did wrong and do it right next time. What is important is the opportunity to keep working and getting new clients and new matters. As long as we have that, we have hope. As long as we have hope, we do not stand still. We do not die.'

When a lawyer does not perform well, the pattern of the firm is to assign blame and to determine guilt or innocence. Both of these patterns create anxiety in the lawyers and inhibit their ability to contribute effectively to the success of the practice group and the firm. When one of my group of lawyers does not live up to expectations, or the clients are not getting the quality of service they expect and pay for, it's my job to identify the problem and help the lawyer fix it. A law firm typically is viewed as a business environment, requiring cool deliberation, decisive action, and direct conversation based on circumspect analysis and good business sense. There is not a lot of focus on feelings in this context."

A team develops

"I need to break the pattern of blame and determining guilt or innocence. I also need to put myself in others' shoes, see things from their perspective, and lead by example.

I will try to identify problems or shortcomings and bring them to each individual lawyer's attention. It is important to make sure the lawyer knows she or he did something wrong. Then I need to help her or him to realize what she or he must do to solve the problem and make sure it does not happen again. I will also need to inform my supervisors of the plan. When one of my group's lawyers — a partner or an associate — falls short in performance, I see it as, in part, a problem in my management and training. I talk with the lawyer involved along the lines of 'Let's analyze what went wrong to see what can we do better next time.' Then, I take appropriate action to provide what is missing. Depending upon the relative position of the lawyer involved, I may involve other lawyers in the discussion. I firmly believe in team play. When one of my team players falls down, the entire team is affected and needs to learn from the experience.

To secure my group's support, I will tell them, 'A successful enterprise requires vision, articulation of a clearly conceived business mission, and leadership.' I want this practice group to be a team with the players helping each other. Our firm's policy is to keep our doors open to each other when anyone needs help. When we lose a case, a client, or achieve a result that was not satisfactory, we will ask, 'What can we learn and what can we do better next time?' Change and adversity represent positive challenges and opportunities for individual and corporate growth. The key is to identify opportunities and use them to the best advantage. Inclusion and open discussion among all those involved is key. The legal structure and obligations of a partnership help to achieve this policy."

An ultimate dimension

"Only occasionally can I imply an ultimate dimension. This is not something that most people are used to dealing with in the workplace, so I pick my moments. When the opportunity arises, I say things like, 'We are blessed to have this happen.' This reference raises eyebrows but it makes the point — perhaps not as forcefully and faithfully as I would like — and it hints at something beyond us.

About the most I can hope to get across is suggested by these words that I include in introductory sessions with new people in our practice group: 'Our work is hard. Spiritual help can make a difference. At a recent leadership training conference of the firm, one of the speakers, a renowned psychologist, talked about star performers and why they often fail so spectacularly. Among other reasons, he identified a lack of humility — a failure to recognize something greater than oneself. He said it was important for everyone to have a relationship with God and be involved in a place of worship — outside the trophy-adorned walls of one's office.'"

Stress leaves their faces and their shoulders loosen

Eddie reports that his vision of helping each other has been received well. He refers to it during both group business planning sessions and one-on-one discussions in the course of working on client matters. Both partners and associates show their acceptance of it by talking and listening. "They like it when something does not go well and I or my partners step forward and say, 'The lawyer [partner or associate] did well. We just got a bad result.' They feel protected and secure that they are not scapegoats. You can see the stress go out of their faces and their shoulders loosen up."

He notes that there is a tendency among lawyers to become anxious about "contemplating one's navel." As he puts it, "While all lawyers practice psychology on one another and on their clients, we do not like too much introspection. It makes us uncomfortable."

Eddie has to follow through on the new policy. He comments, "The associates are anxious when we look at errors and mistakes, and some try to put the responsibility back on me. If some of it is my responsibility, I say, 'That is partly my responsibility. But you still own a part of it.' Many times, if I am willing to shoulder at least some of the blame, they will acknowledge that they have some. I have one associate, in particular, who is very thin-skinned and is not willing to accept a lot of responsibility but has been, slowly but surely, coming around in some good ways. She is more open. She shares information that, previously, she would have kept to herself. She shows more candor and willingness to work extra time and put forth extra effort when required. This policy does work. Reactions to it depend on how high the stakes are and whether somebody perceives that they could be hurt in their career. And, the policy works with the partners who may be part of things not going well."

Eddie has recommended churchgoing directly only one or two times in fifteen years. Both times, he was talking with people to whom religion was already important. His practice group co-chair was brought up in a very religious Jewish household and he observes the Jewish holidays. They respect each other and both are spending more and more time with their families. He jokes, "Yes, we are losing lots of sleep! We call it 'short-term pain for long-term gain.'" The team knows that both for him and for his co-chair time with family is part of their religious conviction.

Roof jumper to MC

Eddie is married and has two sons, fourteen and ten. Eddie's religious story is one of lifelong, mostly satisfying, experiences in church life. The oldest of four in a clergyman's family (with a long history of clergy forebears), he recalls the church buildings and grounds as his first childhood play yard — e.g., hiding in the pews and behind the altar, sneaking jumps off the roof of the church hall, and sledding on the church hill. On Sundays and church holidays, parishioners and other guests often came for dinner, beginning with cheese and crackers and wine or cocktails for the adults. Guests included members of the congregation and clergy from other countries and races. Conversation was always church-centered but frequently ranged into socioeconomic discussions. Communion for men and boys on Washington's Birthday meant good pastries and a sign of admission to the male adult world.

Confirmation in the early teens was a "drag." Eddie chose to stay the course because of his father's role and his mother's steadfast support of that role. He still liked being part of the ceremony of the liturgy as an acolyte and, from age eighteen on, as a licensed lay reader. His trumpet led to playing in a Catholic rock mass, which yielded a trip to New York City to see the taping of the "Tonight Show" and a chance to play one of Doc Severenson's horns. Eddie also had a small job setting up tables for the bridge club that met weekly in the church hall. A Jewish family, whose house he was painting to earn money for college, invited him for a Seder. One of his closest high school friends was Jewish, as were a number of his girlfriends. This led to a closer examination of and contemplation about the Old Testament. At college, the campus church program did not speak to him and he found his way to a nearby seminary for occasional worship.

Eddie became engaged to be married shortly after college. His wife-to-be came from an active and positive church relationship in a different denomination, so the only question was where they would participate. They went to an Engaged Encounter weekend (a weekend led by married couples who share their insight and faith about Christian marriage), making new lifelong friends. The birth of their first son forced the issue of choosing a congregation, because both Eddie and his wife, Mary, wanted their children to have a strong church upbringing. They chose a church that, for each, represented the best of what their childhood churches had offered. Eddie sang in the choir, served as a lay minister, and held various leadership positions. Ten years later, however, he and the family left the congregation when they stopped feeling fed.

Since joining a new congregation, Eddie has resumed his high school love of acting, both in adult dramas and children's pageants, sometimes with one or both sons. From time to time, he MC's programs, shares round robin Sunday school teaching with his wife, and continues his lay reading. He would like to do more, but his work and helping in his sons' scouting programs so far have made it impossible. His wife, however, has become much more involved, and recently was elected to a three-year term as an auditor for the congregation.

A praying lawyer

Eddie picked up his ethics from the Bible, his family experiences, and scouting as a youth. He particularly recalls the New Testament, the Ten Commandments, and the Golden Rule, "In everything do to others as you would have them do to you, for this is the law and the prophets" (Matt 7:12). His key convictions include turning the other cheek and the importance of having a sense of and fulfilling one's mission, while remembering that the things one person does are not all that great in the grand scheme of things. This life is just a preface to another. Eddie observed his parents do their best to treat him and his siblings equally, to listen to the needs of and provide help to others, and to discuss frequently the likely effect of their contemplated words or actions. Participating in church social service activities (e.g., painting an inner city tenement) and Boy Scout activities strengthened his belief that serving others is the highest calling. Eddie likes to point to the Scout Oath, by which a Scout promises to do his best to do his duty to God and his country. At present, Eddie serves as scoutmaster of his older son's troop and as leader of his younger son's den. He observes that, somewhat reflective of the Trinity, duty to God is one of three parts of the Oath, and is emphasized in the twelfth point of the Scout Law: a Scout is reverent. The other eleven points are that a Scout is trustworthy, loyal, helpful, friendly, courteous, kind, obedient, cheerful, thrifty, brave, and clean — what he calls "watchwords for an ethical existence."

Eddie recalls that early in his life, he came to be mindful of the need for divine help and the need to ask for it. For example, he finds himself praying at the outset of each business trip on a plane, "Grant that we may all on board come to know and to do your will." Even more, he prays this kind of prayer before beginning an important hearing or trial. These learnings and habits came as much from observing his mother's and father's actions as from observing their words.

Eddie sees ethics as the rules by which one conducts her/his life. He would say that he gleaned his ethics from the New Testament and his parents' conduct of their own lives. He regards his personal observations as derived from this biblical and familial base. Eddie firmly believes he is a sinner with feet of clay, who needs the promise and gift of forgiveness to renew his life each day. He tries to do works that, as he likes to put it, "glorify his Father in Heaven." ✦

Chapter 4 — In the Local Community

Susan: A Mission in Community Rehabilitation

Officials elected to local government have unusual chances to serve their constituents. As a member of the city council, Susan works to rebuild the homes and quality of life in her district of San Bernardino, California.

I cannot not do it

Susan came to believe local government was the only place where elected officials live among the people they serve. Further, she had always wanted to struggle for what people need. As Susan tells it, "You are their neighbor, not removed from them as their legislator. You are truly accountable to the people you represent. Local government actually tries to respond on a more individual level to the needs in that community. San Bernardino has major problems of urban decline. The people needed effective representation."

When the ward's council member announced he would not seek reelection, Susan believed she could do more than others who might seek the office. She had been an advocate for some projects and a critic of other projects coming before voters. She had won public recognition. Also, for three years, she had chaired the Citizens Advisory Commission, which allocated community development block grants from the federal government for San Bernardino. She decided to run for the ward's seat on the council and to use that role to shape the redevelopment in her ward.

Susan believed running was something she was supposed to do. However, she did not want political office. She shared her reservations with her pastor, who responded that she (the pastor) would have talked her out of it, if Susan had begun by saying she wanted to run. Her minister went on to remind Susan that she was the sole support of her family, that she was doing graduate work, and that she ran her own business. Susan replied, "I know. I believe it will be insane. However, I feel God is calling me to do this. It is something I cannot not do." "Then you have to do it," her minister answered. This growing conviction about being called made Susan decide to run in the face of the logical considerations that said not to.

Looking back now, Susan says, "God had been saying there are answers to complex problems but there are no easy answers. It is hard work. Yet, the inspiration from God is do it anyway! It has been gratifying to help people who never expected they could live in a good home that was actually theirs. Many are new immigrants. Isaiah's message is that God (Isaiah 40:30-31) calls us to run, not walk, and to soar with the wings of an eagle. The passage spoke to me, saying 'Don't just think about it. Do it.' This is my sense of God's role in my decision to seek office and all I have done."

Someone to speak for them

San Bernardino lost more than twenty thousand jobs in a decade when most of the major employers moved out. Susan's ward is an old blue collar section of the town. Most of the people lost their homes and absentee ownership is now high. The ward is extremely diverse ethnically. Stabilizing the ward's neighborhoods will take a long time. Easy answers like gentrification are hard to avoid. One plan being considered by the council was to create a 120-acre area with a thirty-acre lake surrounded by town houses in the middle of the ward. This project would, supposedly, solve the high groundwater problem and upgrade the area's housing. Susan saw this idea as a typical redevelopment effort with the people who are most affected not having a voice to speak for them because they are poor, transient, elderly, or renters.

The people needed a long-term community redevelopment project built around them. In particular, they needed a project that would place them in homes of their own that they could afford to maintain. While such projects were available, the people lacked representatives who had the ability to secure such projects for the ward. Someone who saw the opportunity and ministry to speak for them and work on their behalf was needed. As Susan saw it, "The city should move ahead with any project for the right reasons. The project must leave the people not worse off, but better off. The people affected need to be involved at every step in the planning. The project needs to be planned so that a typical resident can say, 'Yes, this was an inconvenience and a bother, but I live in a safer, better community.

People have been concerned about me and I have been dealt with compassionately and lovingly.'"

The old heart of the city coming to life

Susan set about pulling together the county and the city and the United States Department of Housing and Urban Development for a demonstration project. Low income people normally have just enough money for rent. They cannot take on the maintenance or improvements that second owner homes usually need. The project, to be funded by HUD, would rehabilitate about two hundred houses, both single and multifamily. The units — all were 60-80 years old — would have new floors and carpets, new plumbing, new electricity, new roofs, and windows. The structures were to be taken back to the point of new drywalls, if the rebuilding required it. The buyers would get a property they did not have to put any money into besides mortgage payments.

Buyers of the multifamily units would be either local people or rental companies. The property managers of these multifamily units would be trained in maintaining crime-free housing and qualifying renters. They would either practice these crime-free approaches or be shut down by the city's crime-addiction ordinance.

Finally, since all of the homes on the block would be in good condition, people would have one more incentive to become first-time homeowners. First-time buyers are not attracted to one or two rehabilitated houses with others around them in disrepair — run-down, vacant, or occupied by careless tenants or with vacant lots on the street. Low-income people need adequate housing in a place where they would want to buy a house and live in it.

"I hold up the people's vision of the old heart of the city coming to life; redevelopment that places people in homes of their own will encourage them to manage both their homes and their lives better. Adequate housing for low-income people in a place they would want to buy is at the heart of my vision," says Susan.

From the first, Susan knew the task would be one of forming relationships. For example, she would need the trust of her own council members, of all the funding agencies, and of the ward's people themselves. She also turns to some mentors for guidance. One is a state assemblyman with more than thirty years in local government and public service. Two of the appointed commissioners in her ward offer guidance and ideas as well.

They stand with her when she comes under criticism. Once a year, she calls together commissioners and all who have served on ad hoc committees to develop and evaluate options. One option to emerge is setting up neighborhood empowerment councils to provide input on local concerns. Finally, to avoid the appearance of a clique of inner circle advisers, she calls people together for advice and counsel on the basis of the issue at hand. This practice frees people to stand with her on some issues and to oppose her on others. After three years, she observes, "I am learning as I go. Public service on a local level is really a privilege. People think you are important but it is really a service. Your garbage not picked up is my problem. That's the way it is with holding local office."

Susan draws residents of the ward into the work by meeting with them in neighborhood associations, churches, and crime projects with the police. In April 1999, she called a "summit" where the residents discussed their vision for the area. They came up with the need to have an identity as "the old heart of the city coming back to life" and agreed not to promote their own particular organizations. These "summits" created networks so that everyone knew what others were doing. Food pantries learned when others pantries were open, so that each pantry could refer people to another pantry when it was closed.

Major redevelopments call for adequate preparation by the people. The original lake and town housing proposal was reduced to creating only the thirty-acre lake. Even so, this would be a major change. In response, Susan pulled those affected together to discuss the possible dislocation and how it could be integrated into their life. She worked to prepare for such a change, seeing this opportunity as a gift. She called a meeting to discuss it. She cited how the reservoir might offer a river walk and park a block or two from their homes, where they could watch the water, the ducks, or the pedal boats. The people asked that the reservoir not be fenced off so it would be more like a lake. Further, new town houses, hotels, and a commercial center should be downtown, not around the lake. For the "old heart of the city," the lake should be parklike and residential, the people said. At last report, formidable opposition has risen among residents who might be displaced. Some others believed the project should not be built or should be built somewhere else. Yet, there was also an open mind among many of the residents. These people feel that if the compensation and the relocation left them in a better position, they could support it.

When controversy seems imminent, Susan works to find a common ground to draw people together. She spent time with a neighborhood group of mostly older, original owners in what had been a working-class community. They were retired white people in what had become a largely Hispanic neighborhood. The retirees wanted the community to look the way it did before. Susan told them that they could not just stay in their homes phoning each other to complain. Instead, they must get involved with the newcomers so that the newcomers would be more ready to work with them to establish standards for the quality of life in the neighborhood.

Next, she asked the retirees to volunteer to be part of a youth account-ability board to work with the new families. On such a board, there would be opportunity for positive interaction. This would help the older resi-dents come to see the many issues the newcomers face, many with more pressing problems than keeping their yards trim. She reminded the older residents that they have gifts to offer the newcomers. They raised children here so they know what the newcomers need to do to build a healthy community. On the other hand, the children of the newcomers can restore a needed vitality to the community. Over the eighteen months since Susan recommended it, four older residents have begun to serve on the youth board.

A recent meeting of homeowners preparing for the rehabilitation of their block was convened at St. John's. The church is on that block. The priest, a warden, and another member were there. As people introduced themselves, the church group said, "We're from the church. We are part of the neighborhood and we are so glad you asked to use our hall. You can come back anytime." The church has been repainted and is, thus, another asset to the area.

Incentive to stay

It took two years to get through the contract negotiations for the reha-bilitation project. In October 1999, the city executed and signed off on the contract. Several days later, Susan took the contract before the County Board of Supervisors for their sign-off. Now, in an area four blocks wide and five blocks long — which includes the church she belongs to — the project will buy from the federal government at a 50 percent discount all of the two hundred houses foreclosed by HUD. The homes will be offered to people with incomes less than 80 percent of the median income. The down payment is forgiven if they stay in the home and pay off the thirty-year mortgage. If they sell the home before the mortgage is paid off, the down payment has to be part of the selling price and paid back. Thus, they have an incentive to stay, to pay off the mortgage, and to become anchors in the community.

As part of the rehabilitation plan, the new owners will be taught how to care for their homes — how to cut the grass, how to be part of a neighborhood association, how to keep the neighborhood safe. They will be given the tools to succeed. A local chapter of a nationwide, nonprofit, twenty-year-old organization, Neighborhood Housing Services, will run a home buyer education program. The cost of the education program will be met by funds secured by the district's representative in Congress.

Belief expressed in service

"I know the people I work with so I bring God in whenever I am talking with those to whom religion is vital. I say, 'I am as aware as you are that what we are doing is God's work.'"

Further, Susan pushes the city to partner with religious-based community organizations because they are some of the strongest assets in the community. "If the city wants to deal with community issues, religious communities are one of the places where it should be dealing with these issues. The city is bringing these people to the table more often than it used to," Susan notes.

"The most valuable way that I can share the gift and blessing of belief is to live it out there in the community. It is also the most gratifying way to use it. Singing, worship, and meditation are great, but they are not enough. While many people out there believe in a higher power, they are not necessarily in a church."

Susan came out of the radical Episcopal ministries at the University of Wisconsin in Madison. Jane Fonda met with them. There, Susan learned to be careful about sharing her spiritual beliefs. "Today," she says, "it is not so risky to talk your faith with those with whom you share the same social beliefs. People are more open about belief today. There are very few people you bomb out with when you talk that way today. You can accomplish more because more people today are apt to value that you are a believer."

She does not try to draw them into church life so much as to draw them into service based on the conviction that belief in something greater than yourself is best expressed in the service of others. She does not talk a lot to others about how being in a church can be of support, even though she, herself, finds this support very real.

New solutions

As a council member of San Bernardino, California, Susan helps to govern a city of two hundred thousand. Her work is voluntary with a very modest monthly stipend. She receives about $700 per month to cover expenses. Her expenses are far above the $700 allowance. She has two sons, eighteen and twenty-one, who are away at school. A sixteen-year-old daughter is at home. She has been separated from her husband for two years but has supported the family for more than a decade. For fifteen years, she was the sole proprietor of a contracting business making a steady, sizable income. She began to reflect that this was not using all of her talents and that she did not want to do this for the rest of her life. She wanted most to make San Bernardino a more just and loving environment. While still working full-time in contracting, she began work for an undergraduate degree in environmental studies. In the midst of all this, she ran for office as councilman for her part of the city and won in 1997. In January of 1999, she closed the contracting business and began a new job. She became a water policy analyst for a company that develops new solutions to California's continuing search for water for its growing population. Her college work and her role as a council member were important factors in being offered the new job. Finally, in June of 1999, she received her degree in environmental studies.

Susan grew up in an Episcopal Church in Milwaukee. After a lapse in her twenties, she resumed church participation when she and her husband had children of church school age. They believed church participation would be good for them and for their children. Her husband led the family to a church similar to the fundamentalist church that he had left during his college years. However, the family did not fit in well because her husband found the new church also rigid and judgmental. At that point, they dropped out of participation in any church. Susan did not return to church life until 1995 when a new rector came to St. John's in San Bernardino. Susan had visited St. John's once, before the minister's arrival, but it did not attract her enough to return. Then, she saw a picture in a newspaper of the new minister sitting in her van with baggies of food for the hungry. The paper told how the church members had supplied her with the bags and how members stayed at the church to give out baggies and water when people came in hungry. The baggies were thoughtfully done — even including a napkin. Susan phoned that day and worshiped there from then on. As Susan puts it, "The leader defined a ministry and I decided my ministry fitted in too."

The longest bridge

Susan values worship but emphasizes that faith must be lived out in deeds. She admired, respected, and felt the deep spirituality of activists who fought for social justice — Martin Luther King, Jr., Gandhi, and other such leaders in the fifties, sixties, and seventies. These were people of faith to her. There was also James Groppi, the nationally famous Roman Catholic priest, who led marches on Sunday afternoons across what he called "the longest bridge in the world, the bridge from Africa to Europe." The bridge was the Sixth Street viaduct over an industrial valley in Milwaukee where Susan lived. Blacks lived on the north side of the bridge, whites on the south side. Black people did not buy houses or live on the south side; they did not even go there. So, Fr. Groppi led open housing marches on Sunday afternoons from the north to the south side, over the bridge. They were met with curses and fruit was thrown at them. As a teenager, Susan marched in Fr. Groppi's open housing marches — much to the shame of her parents. She believes she was fortunate to have grown up in Milwaukee in the sixties where she saw and experienced hatred and injustice.

Susan believes God speaks to us by giving us the desire to be in a certain place at a certain time. As she sees it, "People who say they do not know where God is leading them or what God really wants them to do, often do not recognize God's presence in what they want to do. If what they want to do is an honorable, giving thing, then God is speaking to them. God speaks to us very loudly and very strongly." For Susan, God does not come with trumpets or on clouds. She says, "When I feel the satisfaction that, gosh, I was able to be in this place at this time and to be part of this struggle for the right thing, that is a deep part of my belief and spirituality. These are the things I am at peace with because I know where they came from."

A critical mass

Susan learned ethics from being born a baby boomer and coming into adolescence when the issues of racism and war were in the spotlight. At thirteen, she was opposed to racism and unnecessary military violence. She considers it a blessing to have lived through the sixties. She had good parents but they were very conservative. She ascribes her move from a more personal to a more social ethic to the society-wide movements of the day. She was proud to be an Episcopalian because the Episcopalians in Wisconsin were involved in civil rights and antiwar movements. But, her childhood church was not involved in these issues.

During college on both the Milwaukee and Madison campuses, she frequented the places where the Episcopal Church's ministry was carried on — centers with a chaplain living upstairs. These centers were gathering places for social ministry. When she saw the Episcopal name on a poster for an antiwar rally, she decided to check it out and, finding what she agreed with, she stayed. She was gratified to find there were other Episcopalians like her.

During her college years, Susan learned by doing to apply her ethics. She learned about group process and that consensus building had to be the basis for action. She learned ways to find common ground with others to get a critical mass of people to agree. Whether in civil rights, or among welfare rights mothers, or in the antiwar movement, activists wanted a role in the decision-making process and not to leave the decisions to the elected leaders who would tell them what to do. She was lucky enough to have been there when the experiments of getting into the decision-making process were taking place. There were no models for it or real training. Later on, Susan and her colleagues trained people in how to build consensus and how to work through a committee, putting her ethics into practice. ✦

Kevin: A Mission to Support a Community Service Organization

Community programs for youth need adults as both helpers and recruiters. Kevin supports a sisterhood, Job's Daughters, in its work of community service and in building well-being and stability among its members who are maturing from their early teens to young adulthood.

Something more

"I joined the Masons when I moved to Wisconsin. I had learned about the Masons from a friend in England. After my wife and I went to several dinners sponsored by Masons, I wanted to do something more. I was not doing enough for other people. It was one thing to help the church in its physical situation, but you have to stretch out to the community.

Like any good Christian and Mason, I believe in the good that organizations devoted to human welfare can achieve. Growing up, I learned that people who give to and care about their fellow human beings are an asset to society. The Masonic organization for young girls, Job's Daughters, is devoted to human welfare. They strive to support others, especially those in real need. Incidentally, the requirement for joining Job's Daughters that one be related to a Mason is often met with the help of adult advisers who work with candidates to find a Mason somewhere in their background.

I see four problems in our community. We have people in need whom existing programs do not reach. We have prejudice. And, many young girls eleven to twenty lack concern for their own community. Too many of them lack confidence in themselves as leaders who can do something to help others.

Job's Daughters has a fund to help the hearing impaired, HIKE, Hearing-Impaired Kids Endowment. This fund responds to Jesus' teaching to 'love your neighbor as yourself' (Mark 12:31). Our local chapter of Job's Daughters, with other chapters in our state, raises thousands of dollars each year for HIKE. The local chapter, called a bethel, raises money through car washes, bake sales, making and selling Christmas decorations, selling entertainment coupon books, and making and selling sandwiches for Super Bowl Sunday. They also serve at church suppers and, generally, try to help out when they are asked.

Job's Daughters works to eliminate prejudice. Members need only believe in a higher being. Like the Masons, Job's Daughters tries to help their members become better citizens. Members of Job's Daughters show real concern for others and the community at large in their giving and their readiness to help others when asked. The organization increases a sense of well-being and stability in its members and it builds confidence in public speaking and in a girl's own leadership ability.

The oldest of my three daughters joined Job's Daughters at age eleven. When she joined, she was very shy. By the time she finished, she had become the leader of all Job's Daughters in our state, traveling extensively throughout the country. She had become both self-confident and supportive of community-minded activities. My next two daughters followed suit. Job's Daughters also helped the younger of the two grow in confidence and become the Honored Queen (leader of her bethel) with its 35-40 members.

My own role in Job's Daughters has been serving as a liaison between the local bethel and other Masonic organizations. Helping this organization work has been a way for me to do something, through the girls, to help needy people, combat prejudice, and aid young girls to grow in self-confidence and good citizenship."

Drawing others in

"I think people should be more giving and more understanding of each other. I encourage others to follow this way. I have a vision of a world in which people work toward an improved way of life for others. That means better health care. That means knocking on someone's door and letting that person know that help is guaranteed. Church members need avenues other than the church to help people. I drew in my three daughters by talking this way with them and trying to live this way at home.

When asked what she would say to encourage a friend to become a Jobie, my youngest daughter replied, 'I would probably tell her how much being a Jobie helped me. Before I joined Jobies, I was pretty shy. I did not like talking to people. I hated speaking in front of groups of people. Now, I have gained a whole ton of self-confidence and I feel a lot better about myself.'

I believe people need to see worthwhile reasons for doing these things. Those worthwhile reasons are love of God and love of fellow man. God is at work in Job's Daughters in their concern for others. We talk about God all the time. I see nothing wrong with talking about God in any situation. In my opinion, some working belief in God is essential to leading a good life. You have to work at this with care, though. At first, talk of God can frighten some people so you bring them along and allow them to become absorbed at their own pace.

Job's Daughters regularly includes prayer and reading from the Bible at meetings. In our bethel, we talk about a more Christian way of life. Still what really matters is belief in a supreme being.

We encourage our daughters to go to church and we point out that Job's Daughters is not secular; we pray to God in the ritual. Often, the reaction people have to church is entirely different from the reaction they have to Job's Daughters. In school, prayer is suppressed. God and prayer are suppressed by other people because belief in God is not cool and it is not cool to go to church. But it is cool to go to Job's Daughters so, in fact, Job's Daughters assists the work of God. We say the bread and the cup of the church provide support and signify the strength of God in both environments."

A feeling of community

"My wife and I were brought up with the value of serving others. Both of us were in scouting. Scouting got us into community service. It was natural for my wife to join me in supporting Job's Daughters. I recruited others to help by showing them how much good Job's Daughters was doing for the community. When people feel they are helping others, it makes a big difference in how they react.

In like manner, all of our three girls were in Girl Scouts. They joined Job's Daughters as they got older. To get them to join, I took them to a 'Friends' Night.' They got a feeling for the community those girls provided. The oldest gave it a go. Once she started, she began to come out of herself and become more mature. We did relatively the same with the younger two daughters.

My daughters do not always go to church. My oldest daughter, Anne, at twenty-three, goes to church with us occasionally. When she is not nursing on a Sunday, she finds her way to church on her own. My next daughter, Elizabeth, at twenty, is whimsical. She does not always follow through. She does work on Happening. After the ordination of a woman who had worked in Happening, she said, 'You know, I really should go on for confirmation classes.' Once home, she seemed to forget all about it. She believes but she does not always follow through. For my youngest, Martha, at fifteen, being in church on Sunday often depends on whether or not she was up late the night before. She has been to New Beginnings and Happening and is working on the next Happening weekend."

Tough issues to face

Kevin, an engineer by background, is now in sales to increase his income. His company builds induction heating equipment for heat-treating and heating prior to forging and metal melting. He describes himself by saying, "When I take anything on, my competitive nature leads me to take it on as a challenge. I give seminars in my business and have a firm belief in and understanding of what I am talking about. I have no problem standing and talking before five hundred people at a time."

Kevin's wife, Lillian, works for the immunization section of a neighboring town's health department. Their oldest daughter, Anne, lives on her own. Elizabeth, aged twenty, lives at home and is taking classes and working. The youngest, Martha, is in the ninth grade. Kevin has always been part of the church. In England, where he grew up, he would be there when only five others were present. When his parents worked abroad, he attended a Christian boarding school from age seven on. Nurtured by a good faculty and worship every morning, he came to love the church. Though enthusiastic about the church choir, he disliked Sunday because that day was filled with practicing or singing someplace.

He observes, "I never dropped away because there were times in my life when I needed the support and the belief. I needed God and everything I could lay my hands on. There were tough issues at the time. My mother died after two years of illness when I was twenty-one. I married the next year and my wife and I found ourselves responsible for my younger brother of sixteen and sister of fourteen. My father had left the country. My brother was into drugs. My sister could never keep a job. I would promise folks she would do well and, when she would let me down, my credibility was at stake. I ended up in church praying a long time as I wondered what to do next. By the way, after many years of not seeing eye to eye, my father I have reconciled our differences."

When Kevin came to the United States in 1978, he quickly joined the congregation in his neighborhood. He comments, "I found it to be a self-made church with four to five millionaires in the congregation. They wanted for nothing. I sang in their large choir. However, it was not what I was really looking for. When my company moved to the Chicago area, I found a little mission church that had limited resources. In two years, we were able to achieve parish status through hard work in leading people to donate money and time and effort. We had to help people to see worthwhile reasons for doing these things. That worthwhile reason is love of God and love of fellow man."

At present, Kevin teaches a group of 3-6 sixth through eighth graders in his congregation on Sundays. He is also the lay director for Happening (a weekend conference for tenth through twelfth graders for Christian information) in the diocese.

No sudden revelation

For Kevin, a solid foundation in life with God as its source is basic. "To me, religion is a very stable source for managing one's life. I came to these beliefs through my school upbringing where my teachers were believers. God helped me with problems like my sister and brother." Kevin finds, "God gives peace of mind and understanding. Yet, you, also, have to give back to life."

Kevin's core values are the commandments. For him that means "turn the other cheek; be your brother's keeper; don't make fun of your brother or take advantage of him; love your neighbor." Kevin acquired the foundation for his faith and ethics through his early years in that private school in England. He comments, "Without that time in the school, I don't think I would have these thoughts. It is strange that, today, schools suppress religious activity. Most of us do not know how to talk about what we believe in and how to connect belief with the scientific world we live in. It is very difficult to connect belief and science when your belief is not firm. It was difficult for me, initially. Firm belief got me over it. If you are unsure of something, you do not talk about it much. My belief came through no sudden revelation. It came over time. It came from working with people who have similar faith and similar thoughts. Wherever you go, you can meet people with solid conviction. Yes, I probably do seek them out." ✦

Chapter 5 — In the Wider World

Gloria: A Mission in Ethno-mathematics

Teachers who are sensitive to cultural diversity can make learning math easier for their students. Gloria helps people of all ages to overcome cultural barriers that block their learning in mathematics.

Blocks to learning math

"The comfortable decide for the uncomfortable yet remain socially removed from them. In this way, inequitable social systems persist, globally. For example, a large portion of the population is unable to learn mathematics as it is taught in school. Yet, they recognize that math is something they should know. As a mathematics teacher, I cannot imagine that God is satisfied with this situation. Nor do I believe that mathematical knowledge is possessed only by an elite corps of individuals.

The problem seems to be how math is presented in school. Alan Bishop, a mathematician, has identified at least six basic human activities from which mathematics is derived — counting, measuring, locating (from directions to geometry), playing (Michael Jordan uses geometry and trajectories to make basketball shots), designing (from the elbow of a pipe to the heel of a sock), and explaining (mathematical logic using both deductive and inductive reasoning). Every cultural group answers the questions of how many? How much? How far? and How long? In other words, every cultural group has its own way of doing mathematics. Therefore, if mathematics is presented to one cultural group in the terms used for mathematics by another cultural group, their learning is likely to be inhibited. Discovering and comparing the various ways in which mathematics is presented in different cultures has come to be known as ethno-mathematics; this does not mean ethnic-mathematics. All identifiable cultures — the cultures of farmers, bankers, engineers, athletes, carpenters, medical doctors, and physicists — have their own mathematical language, instrumentation, techniques, scholars, and literature.

Many teachers are unaware of how culturally conditioned they are. For example, I was asked to edit a math textbook from the ethno-mathematical stance. The editor had in mind counting racial groups to make sure the material was inclusive enough for U.S. classrooms. I found a Ferris wheel — a cultural artifact — used to introduce a mathematical problem. I knew that many children would not know what a Ferris wheel is. If a mathematical model of the amusement ride was to be used, it should be accompanied by a picture and a description of what the ride is like.

Inequality arises when the teacher is not aware that culturally different students approach mathematics differently. It is like teaching a subject in English when the students understand only Japanese. The students know the concepts but do not know them in English. For example, some Haitian friends gave me some directions — a basic mathematical activity — using the words 'pass the expressway.' I could not tell if they meant go over the expressway or alongside it. This created 'mega confusion.'"

Math for all

"To increase a person's mathematical ability, teachers need to be culturally literate. Teachers become culturally literate by sharing freely their time and attention with their students. As you listen with care, you are letting the culture of another person point to the peculiarities of your own culture. We learn to ask a class, 'How do you do it in your home?'

Students in mathematics could learn a lot more easily by working with their neighbors. This is how I learned mathematics — in a sharing mode. As children and youths, my friends and I sat around the dining room table to do our homework. We were encouraged to work together. I helped in mathematics, while others helped in areas in which they were good. Further, in math, your group helps you to know whether or not you are right. Mathematician Andrew Wiles claimed to have proved Fermat's last theorem — a problem that had not been solved for three hundred years. He presented a paper. But he had not had it reviewed by peers. About five months after he presented his paper, others began to discover the glitches in the proof he offered. It took nine months for people to fill in the gaps in Wiles' proof. You work in a group not to show off but to get others' input into what you are doing. Too often, we tell students to work alone. They would do better if they studied often in groups. As a teacher, during the first week of class, I created study groups and each student was in one.

Beyond the classroom, I served as director of a national program called 'Blacks and Mathematics,' which was sponsored by the Mathematical

Association of America (MAA). MAA wanted to increase the number of minority students preparing for careers in mathematics. As the second national director, I suggested more students would be attracted to mathematics if they knew some of the interesting applications of math. We found math teachers in colleges who would go into high schools and teach applications of math.

For example, when trying to teach some high schoolers about probabilistic reasoning, I challenged students who claimed to be able to distinguish between two similar soft drinks. They were given five trials. We looked at the probability of a person without a perfected sense of taste being able to choose correctly. Initially, students assumed that if a person did not achieve a perfect score, then that person had no sense of discrimination between the two soft drinks. Upon learning how unlikely it is for one to get four correct in five trials by chance alone, students understand why small errors are tolerated in experiments of this type. In this way, high school teachers learned along with their students, and we left literature for them on similar interesting applications of mathematics.

In 1984, while working for the federal government, I went to a conference in Australia and heard Ubiratan D'Ambrosio, the 'father' of ethnomathematics, talk about his work. He described how people in a given culture do a lot of mathematical things without understanding that math is involved. For example, they may make a fishnet or a basket without understanding the school math behind it. Geometry and optimization of volume and strength are part of making baskets and fishnets. People making the first fishnets or baskets understood the mathematical principles at work as they created them. Often, others learned the process by imitation.

Captivated by D'Ambrosio's insights, I then began to look for other people working this way. Paulus Gerdes in Mozambique said mathematics was frozen in the artifacts people make. He took the artifacts apart to see that they were not randomly put together but that a lot of mathematics had gone into them. The writings of Allen Bishop of Australia also helped me. He said that every cultural group has its own ways of 'mathematizing.' I popularized Bishop's work by giving talks around this country and by helping doctoral students use these activities as the focus of their dissertations. I began to find math in the strategies used in people's games; in the logic they used to explain things; and the things they designed and measured without instruments. I began to see one could learn a people's mathematics by studying the things that occupy their lives.

A year after that meeting with D'Ambrosio in Australia, we formed the International Study Group on Ethno-mathematics and I became the first president. I began to study and to write and to strengthen the organization. We now have sections in North America, Brazil, and Argentina. In all my travels, I seek to learn in what ways God communicates mathematical knowledge to people with different gifts. Then I share this knowledge with groups to expand their understanding and interest in mathematics. When I tell Ubiratan he is the 'father' of ethno-mathematics, he says, 'If I am the father, you are the mother.'

When I meet teachers who have no understanding of ethno-mathematics, I challenge them by asking what they know of 'the mathematics of the people' — the people who lay carpets, who design things, and who cook. I talk with them about Bishop's six basic activities in mathematics. They begin to realize that they use mathematics in ways they themselves as teachers of mathematics did not even recognize outside the classroom. Then, they begin to learn that people in every culture have their own way of doing mathematics. They begin to ask their fourth graders how they do things at home and begin to point out the mathematics they are using. The fourth graders learn they are important because what they do is talked about in the classroom. Moreover, they can use the mathematics they are learning right now. They are not learning something now just so they can learn calculus in college.

The story is told of how an older student became interested in the mathematics he had previously hated when asked to bring his hobby into class. His hobby was flying pigeons. Class discussion brought out how his hobby involved distances, locating, and weighing the pigeons – all associated with mathematical ideas. You will not get the attention of students until you get close enough to them to know what they do in their lives. You respect the students' knowledge first and then you expand how they see the world and how mathematics helps them to see more of it.

The teachers become highly motivated as they learn to appreciate cultural differences. They begin to teach better and the students begin to learn better. I also invite anyone I know to attend conferences where they will meet people in ethno-mathematics and to attend ethno-mathematics sessions. I encourage them to present papers on what they have learned to their colleagues back home."

God and math in the same breath?

"I have to be very careful about talk of God when I am working in ethno-mathematics. To talk of God would go beyond the bounds of the profession. Instead, I point to God by encouraging actions that imply human limitations. I talk about the importance of sharing; respecting other people's knowledge; and acknowledging how other people think without jumping to conclusions about what they know. For some in mathematics, talking of God explicitly would suggest you are leaning on religion because you have nothing else to say. On the other hand, I do talk of God with my spiritual friends in ethno-mathematics.

I believe that talk of God's work in ethno-mathematics in church circles takes a special approach. Once I was asked to give a talk in my church on my work in ethno-mathematics. I had only twenty minutes to speak so I told of how church people who were in mathematics formed me and my interest in mathematics. Then, I told of how God gives us different ways of knowing as a rationale for my profound interest in ethno-mathematics.

The typical congregation does not appear to be interested in justice ministries. To open up understanding of institutional racism, I gave my bishop a book called *Indicators of Racism, Sexism, and Classism* (National Council of Churches of Christ, 1992). He purchased one hundred copies for me to sell across the diocese. Often, church workers among poor people in underdeveloped countries seem to perpetuate dependency by meeting only physical needs and not teaching people the skills they need to manage their own lives.

When a friend lost his job in math, I suggested to him, 'This was God's way of saying to you that you have done His work here and it is time to move on to something new.' While it took time for him to move on, he kept pushing until he found a chairmanship position in mathematics at another university. A young math instructor shared concern for a homeless brother. She, herself, was very bitter about not being paid fairly because of her race. I counseled, 'I have felt that way, but you must move on. Start afresh as I had to.'

People are attracted to me to help them solve their problems. In this process, they share my life, my friends, and my church. I introduce them to others and try to involve them in outreach and justice ministries so that they might solve their own problems."

At home in math

Gloria lives in a condominium complex with 140 families overlooking a man-made lake and a wildlife preserve that is visited by lots of people. She has a married son with two children who lives in Pittsburgh, works as a franchise lawyer, and owns a franchise. Her daughter is single and works as an educational marketing manager for *The New York Times* in that city. During her growing up years, Gloria says her mother told her repeatedly, "When I carried you in my womb, I prayed that you would be a humanitarian." Her father often told her that she would be a doctor. Gloria strove to achieve both expectations. Since her mother was a Baptist and her father was an Episcopalian, she went to both churches until her second year in college. She was baptized and reaffirmed her baptism in adolescence in the Episcopal Church.

Gloria comments, "I find the Episcopal Church lets go of you after confirmation. At twelve, I was growing and learning so many things and then I got stuck there with no more learning experiences set before me by the church. Consequently, I do not know the Bible as my Baptist friends do. I memorized the Apostles' and Nicene Creeds, the Ten Commandments, the Beatitudes, a grace before meals, and prayers upon entering and leaving church. I truly admire people who pray spontaneously. So, when you ask me how I talk of God, it is probably not with words but, rather, with deeds. A friend says, 'You pray, Gloria, but not in conventional ways.'"

Gloria grew up with mathematics as a familiar part of her life. When she was nine, her father opened a grocery store where she worked daily — counting, weighing, and measuring — selling merchandise. Gloria loved to play school and always wanted to be the teacher. Teachers liked her enthusiasm for learning. In fourth grade, her teacher hired her for twenty-five cents a week to tutor kids before the school day began and to grade arithmetic papers. Mathematics and church were linked through her many math teachers who belonged to her Episcopal Church — her algebra teacher, her advanced algebra teacher, and her pastor with a master's degree in mathematics. In college, her calculus teacher had been a Sunday School teacher in her Baptist church.

The international group in ethno-mathematics of which Gloria is a founder kept her as president for more than ten years due to her organizational development skills. In 1996, she left that position. Since then, the group has expanded in the Americas. She is helping with that expansion, especially in Canada.

A journey to justice, power, and peace

"I believe my ministry is to connect people with information that can be transformed into serving God better. My life's journey is to discern how God would have us serve. What guides my journey is a passion for justice. I believe following God is the journey to justice, power, and peace.

I grew up not understanding much about racism. I understood about prejudice and bigotry and lynching but I really did not understand institutional racism. In the sixties, the YWCA taught me about this phenomenon. I joined the YWCA for my children to meet others in a Christian setting and enjoy the benefits of the Y's programs. The Y's leaders identified me as a potential leader. Dorothy Height, now the President Emeritus of the National Council of Negro Women, encouraged me to accept a nomination to the national board of the YWCA. I did so and was elected. They were working on institutional racism and economic development in depressed areas. They taught how institutions channeled privilege and contributed to oppression, often unintentionally. I learned quickly and well!

My growth in learning about the church's concern for justice came along more slowly. I had to be taught about it. After twelve years of age, the only teaching I received came through sermons that almost never focused on the day's news and daily life. I had to live through the congregation's unjust practices such as no children, only adult men, could serve as acolytes. During the civil rights struggle, our diocese, with the help of its Urban Missioner, took a strong role in the civil rights movement. Our Urban Missioner also taught me about the National Episcopal Church and got me involved in the Presiding Bishop's Committee on Evangelism, among other activities.

My pastor, during my time as warden in the late seventies, continued my education about the church in daily life. After preaching, he sometimes stood in the nave of the church while the congregation interrogated him about the sermon. His talk in the aisle was all about what was going on in that city and what was in the newspaper. A neighboring minister took me still further in the early nineties. He asked me to join him in working on issues of racial justice in the Diocese of Milwaukee, where I have continued with that work. I also review social ministry centers of the Episcopal Church.

'As a teacher, I learned to respect other people's knowledge and experience. When you respect people, you give them time and attention. Out of that respect, you learn something of what God is like — the universe is so big and there are so many different people in it and each has so many rich ideas of loving and caring. They represent the faces of God. In the early nineties, I purchased a musical tape of the Prayer of St. Francis of Assisi. I listened to it over and over again, until I finally internalized the concept ' . . . that I may seek not so much to be understood as to understand.' This was a turning point in my life. Now I am not so concerned about myself as about others.

It is very clear to me how God operates in my life. Almost every day, something happens in my life that is connected with what I would like to have happen. This confidence that God is in my life day by day was not always there. I am not sure when it came. It was evolving. If what happens is not what I want, I recall a prayer of my mother, 'God, you are better to me than I am to myself.' I don't know just what I should ask for when I pray; so, I ask for guidance to make the right choices or to support someone or to encourage people. I constantly discover God's work in the opportunities God brings into my life to share the gifts God has given to me. These opportunities come in many ways — a dyslexic fifteen-year-old who wants to learn algebra; a foundation in an impoverished nation seeking a relationship with the church; a stranger in an airport in a problematic relationship with a married man; and an angry math professor who will not receive tenure. Needs that sound personal have mathematical aspects in that they call for the explaining or interpreting the function of mathematics."

Gloria commented on what telling her story here has meant to her: "I am grateful to you for making me unearth a lot of things that have helped me to understand my journey. I am sharing with others how this is done.

Now I see the church as an instrument for advancing justice. Somehow, God alerts me to injustice and I speak out. Of course, many friends ostricize me for this, especially if it rocks their boat. This is a Christian dilemma. But I have concluded that my friends' flight is God's way of having me follow Him and not them!" ✦

Lloyd: A Mission to Oppose the State Lottery

Legalized gambling continues to grow. What used to be an "evil" is, now, read-ily available in food stores and restaurants. Lloyd believes this sea change to be a serious social error. With others, Lloyd opposed the adoption of a state lottery but, since it passed, now works to keep its operation as honest as pos-sible and to modify it where changes could be made.

Opposition rises

"A lottery was proposed for Wisconsin in about 1985. In 1897, the state had become so disenchanted with gambling that it passed an amendment to the constitution prohibiting gambling. Thus, the lottery could become legal only through amending the constitution. I knew from the com-mandment 'Love Your Neighbor' that I had to oppose this action. Before then, I was active in the Center for Community Concerns, a Habitat for Humanity food program, and advocacy for youth in trouble with the law.

By amending the constitution, the state would, in effect, encourage gam-bling. I knew that gambling would put a terrible strain on the poor. Many people would gamble and risk more than they could afford to risk. I also knew that some would become addicted. Another disturbing fact was that more gamblers meant more customers for illegal gambling. New York had found that introducing the lottery led to a fivefold increase in illegal gam-bling in the state. The racketeers attracted betting on the same lotteries by offering bigger payoffs to winners. Then, to offset their own losses when a number received a lot of bets, the racketeers placed bets on the same numbers themselves. Statewide deterioration of community became a very real fear.

I knew that groups must form to oppose gambling legislation. I decid-ed to join a group and do what we could to oppose gambling.

When taxes and rebates were talked about, I pointed out that the prof-its from gambling were much less favorable than gambling's negative effects — increased crime, the need for more police, and the embezzling of funds to finance gambling. I wrote letters to the editor that did receive favorable response. In these letters, I cited gambling's effect on the family — especially, on children. A local grocer stopped selling lottery tickets because he saw parents buying tickets, rather than food for their families.

An elected official confided that, in the past, he gave up gambling when he found he could not afford shoes for his children."

Risking money most people cannot afford to lose — a religious issue?

"Early on, I found that while people could see the lottery as a moral question for individuals and a political question for the community, they were not ready to see the lottery as a religious problem. For many, it was only a political question that should not be brought into the church.

I registered at the local library as a speaker on gambling. The only call came from a group of college women who were holding a drawing for a small gift the night I came to speak. As they laughed about the coincidence, I responded with a definition of gambling that I had picked up from a local clergyman: 'Gambling is not a matter of taking a chance. One takes a chance getting out of bed in the morning. Gambling is risking money that most people cannot afford to lose.' At the end of my talk, one person did respond asking what she could do."

A public hearing with few listening

"The Wisconsin Conference of Churches appointed the Gambling Issues Task Force to oppose the lottery. With the bishop's consent, I volunteered to serve on it as a member from the Diocese of Milwaukee. The task force organized a statewide group, The Coalition to Stop Legalized Gambling. The group took the word 'stop' for their buttons and 'STOP' became their commonly used name. The ecumenical task force became part of STOP. I became the treasurer of the group. Another small group, The Wisconsin Council for Gambling Problems, was formed in Milwaukee.

Working together, STOP and the Council for Gambling Problems gathered the opposition and organized rallies throughout the state. These rallies called on the legislators to vote against the proposal. In response, the assembly appointed an oversight committee to secure public acceptance of the lottery and to hold public hearings around the state for people to make their input to the proposal. The first was held May 20, 1987. During these hearings, opponents of the lottery who described themselves as speaking in behalf of a church body were greeted with catcalls and whistles. When I spoke for the Episcopal Diocese of Milwaukee, a man near me said, 'Do-gooder, go home.' However, these hearings were so well attended that the

Oversight Committee decided it needed to arrange a large public hearing in Madison.

At this time, there was also a push by one group to allow betting on horse racing and by another to allow betting on dog racing. These two groups fought each other assuming that only one kind of racing would be accepted. Further, the work of these two groups drew powerful animal-protective organizations into opposing the lottery legislation.

When the day of the public hearing came, large numbers of gambling opponents were present. Those who wished to speak on the issue signed up for specific times to speak. So many signed up that some people decided that having signed up to speak expressed their opposition sufficiently and chose to leave. The remaining crowd still overflowed the large hearing room. The facts and reasoning presented by the opponents were of high quality. Unfortunately, the members of the Oversight Committee rotated so that only one or two were listening at any one time. At 3:00 p.m., the committee reported to both the senate and the assembly that the hearing was favorable to the lottery while the people at the hearing kept speaking until 5:00 p.m. Many people left with a low opinion of representative government that day.

The majority of the legislature was easy to convince when they were promised huge funds to dispense without raising taxes. The lottery would make it possible to pass some of the largesse on to the taxpayers as a lottery credit — its actual wording — on their real estate tax bills. I recall hearing one man say about his desire for the 'credit,' 'I don't care if it's only two dollars.' Throughout the legislature's consideration of the lottery, advisers from Las Vegas-controlled enterprises guided the legislators in how to set up and to promote passage of the lottery among the voters."

Opponents become monitors

"When it became even more obvious that the bill was going to pass, STOP succeeded in placing a representative in the group drafting the amendment. The representative got two restrictions included in the amendment. One would not permit promotional advertising. The second would allow only on-track betting. The effort proved fruitless. Even though it passed, it was not enforced — either by the Republican governor or the Democratic attorney general. I asked both officials by mail why they did not enforce those provisions. I never received a reply. Once the lottery started, revenues developed losses that none of the state officials seemed to be able to account for. Plus, the Las Vegas-controlled enterprises went on to sell to the state the expensive equipment needed to run the lottery.

The woman who was president of our STOP organization resigned and made clear to us verbally that she did so out of fear of reprisal or actual injury by gambling forces. Efforts to keep STOP together were fruitless, and I made my final report as treasurer to the state Election Committee. A few of us retreated to our small group in Milwaukee to keep some pressure on the legislature. Down to four in number, one of us, using his library connections for research on the legislature, kept us in touch with information we could not get otherwise. To keep pressure on the legislators, two of us kept writing letters to them about problems arising in running the lottery. We also sent a hundred or so copies of each letter to interested citizens. Recently, we objected to plans to finance the lottery through state funds outside the lottery itself. Such state funding would have increased the size of the 'lottery credit' on the real estate taxes. Objections became so strong that the plans were withdrawn and the lottery finances were taken out of the lottery itself. Overall returns from the lottery have been considerably lower than expected. Occasionally, backlash to the lottery arises, but it has never been strong enough to remove it.

When the subject of gambling comes up, I am often the object of good-natured humor. It seems that most of the people are not interested in the lottery per se and say to themselves, 'If some people want to gamble, let them.' They do not seem to realize the lottery's effect on the life of the whole state."

Forestalling Alzheimer's

Lloyd, retired, lives in Racine, Wisconsin, with his wife. They have two daughters and one son. His working days were spent as an electrical engineer in the space and paper industries. Lloyd has been a lifelong participant in congregational life. At about sixteen, he had a brief period of doubt but kept on praying and worshiping regularly. He recalls, "After two or three months, I began to see my prayers were not going into empty space but were somehow being received." Worship has continued to be an important part of his life. He and his wife are at both Sunday and Thursday morning eucharists. Bible study follows the liturgy on Thursdays. He has always felt close to the clergy and was careful to offer them reassurance when he believed it was needed. Having worked up to tithing, he serves on a committee that supports a member who runs an inter-church food and clothing center for low-income people. With tongue in cheek, he comments that community projects forestall the onset of Alzheimer's disease. About ten years ago, he and a few others at the church were talking over a news story about the potential for living to be 120 years old. He recalls, "I joked that I believe I'll live to be a hundred twenty. As I walked away from the group, a calm came over me and a voice said to me, 'You will die soon.' It was said in such a way I had no fear. Instead, I saw that did not mean tomorrow, the next year, or in a couple of years, but rather in God's time, which is measured in eons. My priest agreed this did not mean immediately as in earth terms. I reduced my goal by at least twenty years!"

Part of the vine

Lloyd has always listened closely to sermons and has gained a lot of his biblical knowledge from them. During church school years, fifth graders and up stayed for the full adult sermon and then left for their classes. As one of the acolytes from ten on, he discussed and was part of service projects for people in need carried on with members of the congregation's Brotherhood of St. Andrew chapter. He also visited aging and shut-in people from twelve on.

"I am the vine, you are the branches" (John 15:5) and "Truly I tell you, just as you did it to one of the least of these who are members of my family, you did it to me" (Matt 25:40) guide Lloyd's ethics. His current Bible study group uses *Experiencing God* (Henry Blackaby Ministries, Inc., November 1993; available through Amazon.com), a set of videotapes and discussion guide by Henry T. Blackaby. The group provides for the individual witness Lloyd values. The participants affirm that these two texts are Lloyd's modus operandi.

Lloyd and his associates in opposing gambling find their church life a strong support for strength and direction to carry on the work. For Lloyd, standing up for what you believe in is a Christian principle that gives him "the backbone" to stand up for his convictions regardless of the ridicule or opposition he faces. Two of his priests have used Lloyd as an example of standing up for a principle that is unpopular. ✦

Chapter 6 — In Leisure

Bonnie: A Mission of Family Camping

Careful vacation planning can build family relationships. Bonnie, with the help of her husband, Jim, makes camping a significant part of their ongoing life as a family.

Get away

"As I try to answer this question, I wish I were a deeper Christian. I have a long way to go to think in theological terms easily. I put it this way. God seems to be saying, 'Get away from the stress of everyday life and get back to the basics. Get away from the phone and running into work for a couple of hours just to get some undone things done. You need to regroup and appreciate what you have and what is out there for you.'

My desire to go camping grew over the years. I found myself just wanting to get back to a favorite spot or to find a new one. I love the north shore of Lake Superior north of Duluth, especially Split Rock Lighthouse. I love sitting among the rocks just watching the waves and the kids throwing rocks in the water. I find it very calming and quieting.

I was held back by need for money to take the trip or by letting all the things that need to be done prevent me from getting out. For example, I am off this week and have already planned to fill my time with getting things done around the house, getting tax papers together, and a few appointments.

I just had to go with the need to be together as a family. I need to accept that I cannot get everything done so just go away and enjoy yourself. Our kids are approaching the age where they will no longer want to hang around with us, but would rather be with their friends. I need to take the time off while we can still camp together.

I got my husband to join me in saying to the kids things like, 'Wouldn't it be fun to go to this camp where they have trails like the ones in this picture and we can go visit this place that is nearby?' and 'Wouldn't it be fun to get away from the everyday routine of the house — to be in a different place and do things we usually do not do like building a campfire at night!'"

Campfire talk of God

"God comes up as we sit around the campfire. Our son, Calvin, age thirteen, once said, 'Isn't it something that God made all this. I answered, 'Yes, it is, and we are on just one little speck of land here. Imagine all the other beauty that surrounds us and all the stars in heaven and everywhere else too.' Calvin looked around taking it all in. Kelley, our eleven-year-old daughter, talked the same way saying, 'This sure is pretty — what God made.'

In the past, when I heard others talk, I would think, why don't I talk in those terms where God is right there in the first place, not the second place. There was a wall or something that held me back and I didn't know why. Only in the last year has a big change come over me, and I am trying to explore religion more. In the past, I have not talked of God and church, but I hope as I continue to learn we can discuss things like that more. At Trinity, we have Godly Play for Sunday School. I ask the kids a lot about it to make sure they have been listening and to learn things myself. They tell me of the parable they have talked about. When I say, 'I didn't know that,' I am telling the truth 90 percent of the time."

Bonnie is looking forward in early summer to a family and touring week in the northern peninsula of Michigan. A change in the school schedule prevented such a trip at the end of last summer. She trusts God will be "right there" since God is everywhere.

Campers from the start

Bonnie and her family live in the Minneapolis-St. Paul region. Bonnie works as a human resources administrator. Jim drives for an auto and truck salvage company. In childhood, going to a cabin for two to three days was as close as Bonnie came to camping. Her camping began when she joined the Explorers of the Boy Scouts at seventeen [one of the coed programs for senior scouts]. With the Explorers, she went portaging and canoeing in the Boundary Waters of Minnesota and Canada. She met Jim in the Explorers and they married four years later. After marriage, they occasionally returned to the Boundary Waters with friends. When Calvin came along, they said, "Let's take him even though he is only a year old."

They rented a pop up camper and went to an area in Wisconsin. Calvin toddled around as they sat by the pool. When Kelley arrived, they continued the tradition. The diapers and all the needed gear did not mar their enjoyment. The two children found it to be fun. They took the children's tricycles and, later, their small two-wheelers. As a family, they rode the bike trails of both state and private parks. As the children got older, a bigger camper gave the children their own beds.

Life and worship connect

Bonnie was always an Episcopalian and the family worshiped fairly regularly. However, there was not a lot of talk of God in the home. The Scout leaders kept religious practice alive for her. They led worship every Sunday while the troop was hiking or camping. "It was short but still we did it before heading out on our hiking."

Jim was Lutheran, and he and his brother and mother worshiped now and then. When he and Bonnie married, Jim was a mechanic on a team that raced stock cars on the weekends and Sunday worship fairly well ceased. When Calvin was born, Bonnie said, "You know, it may be time for us to focus on church a bit more." Having lived in their community for eleven years, they noticed, for the first time, an Episcopal Church on a side street. Reading "The Episcopal Church Welcomes You" sign, she thought, "An Episcopal Church right here, two miles from the house!" They became regular Sunday participants and, for the first time, Bonnie began to connect her life with worship.

Bonnie wanted her son to be more than just aware that the church existed. When she asked about baptism, the pastor said, "If you are coming to church just to get Calvin baptized, that is not enough." He was satisfied to proceed when she responded, "We had gone before and just stopped for whatever reasons. Now it is just time to get back." If the children are reluctant on a Sunday, Bonnie simply says, "On Sundays, we go. An hour and a half a week is what we do. You need your religious education and I need it, too — I really do."

Bonnie says of her return to church: "The sermons really touch me. I enjoy the sermons because I learn a lot. One interim priest talked about communion for kids, explaining that it is okay. Also, we had another minister who was very down to earth. He told of his own experiences such as his problems raising his children and how he wondered if he would get through it. When our present minister came, she talked during Lent about the seven deadly sins and related them to daily life. As I mature, I learn more and I want to learn more."

Bonnie uses her learning. When Calvin, at about five, asked, "What is heaven?" she responded, "Heaven is a wonderful place where everyone goes when they die. My two grandpas and grandmas are there. The cat we had to put to sleep is there, running and chasing the rabbits and no longer has the broken leg — she feels good and her body doesn't hurt anymore. And grandpa is not in pain. He doesn't have to take pills anymore." Calvin said, "Oh, okay."

Bonnie served as church treasurer for three years. She passed the job on when she found she was making all of the church's financial problems her own. Jim is now a regular in the Family Table group, which prepares meals for people who use the local food shelves. At first, he went as part of the Boy Scout troop he helps to lead. He has stayed on, made a lot of new friends, and is involved in the church as he never has been before. When prayers for healing are offered during the liturgy, Jim often goes forward for his own healing or for the healing of relatives in need.

At this time, Bonnie says, "I am looking for a better understanding of God and Jesus. A few months ago, we received a survey of the congregation by mail. The survey asked if our needs were being met. I wrote, 'There is an emptiness. I am not happy and I don't know why.' I added my name and phone number. Seeing my name, the minister phoned and we got together. I told her this was a low period in my life. For some reason I was not allowing myself to accept God's love. I said to her, 'I am not the nicest person. Why should God love me?' She answered, 'Bonnie, you are far too hard on yourself.' We talked for only an hour and I left feeling really good. That was a turning point for me and I am still working through it. I begin to see how communion connects with me more than it did before. I can go to be fed with God's love and it is not a judgment. I can pray for help or in thanksgiving. When I receive, it touches me more than it did before."

Right now, family comes first

Talking of her ethics, Bonnie observes, "Respect and honesty in my family are basic. I try to be truthful, as well. For me, right now, my kids and my husband and my parents come first."

Bonnie relates an incident common to many families: "I am working through honesty with my daughter. She brought home some papers I was to look at and sign, and she was to take them back to school. Instead, she signed my name and returned them. I handled this occasion better than I handled the same problem last year with my son. He was having problems turning in his homework. I screamed and yelled and acted like a shrew. I cried for an hour afterwards. This time, the talk with Kelley was serious but there was no yelling. I said, 'Here's the deal. You did this to yourself. I am very disappointed in you. I cannot trust you anymore because you tell me things and I do not know if you are lying or not. It will take time, Kelley, to rebuild that trust.' I did most of the talking but, at least, we were talking. Last week, I caught her lying again. When she finally told me the truth, I said, 'Now I can tell you are telling me the truth.' She dropped her head, 'Yeah.' I went on, 'If you had told me the truth the first time, there would have been some trouble. But to lie about it puts you in bigger trouble. You have to learn that the hard way. But we will get through this.' Things are better now."

Bonnie learned her values at home. "We were a close-knit family — not as close-knit as the Waltons on TV — but we were close-knit. We enjoyed each other, had fun, and went through our share of trials and troubles. Yet, respect and honesty were always there. I also learned a lot from my Scout leaders about respect. They earned my respect for sticking to their values when they were not the most popular. What you saw was the way they were." ✦

Roy: A Mission of Leading a Fly Tying Group

Tying flies is not a popular or highly competitive activity. Yet, minor as it might seem, it can generate activity and form community. Roy leads and teaches a group in tying flies for fishing as a healthy leisure time activity.

Catching each other

"God was telling me to take more leisure time, to share it with others, and to use it wisely. I have a lot of stress in my life — not only from daily living, but also from the demands of work and church. I put pressure on myself and I have it from others. I think that I should be doing more. I often have more leisure time when I travel than when I am home with family, friends, and my church family.

Reading of Forward Day by Day helped me realize I did not have to work myself into the ground to please God or Jesus. Instead, I needed to relax more and listen for God's message to me. As I spent more time outdoors and visiting places I had never seen before, I became increasingly aware of the grandeur of our environment. The blessings God has given astound me. We need to spend more time enjoying the blessings of nature and caring for them. As I read, the division between my religious and my daily life became less and less visible.

I get too involved in the 'world's plan' rather than 'God's plan.' The world tends to lead us into materialism and a hurry-scurry lifestyle. We are seduced. We start to put possessions, career, and climbing the ladder ahead of moral rightness and doing good for others. I still cope with this seduction as do most Americans. In the midst of these pressures, I see the whole process of fishing and enjoying nature's bounty as God's blessing. God has put it there for me to enjoy and to use wisely. Native Americans said a prayer of thanks whenever they killed game in order to survive. While we may say grace over our food, we take so much for granted. At the grocery store, we do not see crops being grown and the labor that goes into harvesting them. We do not see animals being raised and the labor that goes into producing the meat for our tables. We often forget that all we have comes from one great, powerful, benevolent source. It is so easy to get caught up in taking for granted our many gifts, without taking time to focus on giving thanks for all these blessings. I have begun daily prayer in the last year, to help me focus on God's presence and blessings.

I need to make a greater effort to focus on the spiritual part of life. I need to develop more communication with God and more comfort with God than I have now. I want a better understanding of God and how God and Jesus work in my life.

In fly tying, a person has to focus exclusively on what he or she is doing — not only to learn but to teach others. In tying flies, the object is to create something that will entice and catch fish. Further, while people are tying together, they are also catching each other — catching each other's attention and interest and sharing an appreciation of everything connected with fishing. The very relaxation and peace that come while tying flies are part of being closer to God and to Jesus who recruited fishermen to help him.

The minister of the church also fishes and ties flies. In sharing the enjoyment of fly fishing, we talked of Jesus choosing fishermen for several of his disciples. Out of this reflection, I saw the possibility for the church to serve as a meeting place for people who had these same interests. This could foster a sense that the church is a positive place to be at times other than worship. Including nonchurch people in the group seemed to be part of the congregation's mission to share the warm and giving place church can be. We resolved to start a fly tying group at the church that would be open to all interested people.

For myself, I resolved to talk about how tying flies offers time for relaxation in the midst of the busy lives most of us lead. I resolved to talk about the fly tying classes as times of good fellowship — the sharing of feelings and ideas. I resolved to ask God to help me to find gentle ways to invite and to involve people to participate in the spiritual side of life.

I try to avoid pushing my experience of God's love on others. I try to live that love, rather than talk about it as something someone must do. When I fish with a friend or when I offer fly tying instruction, I try to hint at God's blessings in the very existence of fish and water and the like. In the group, I comment on prayer as a powerful force in life. Beyond that, I seek to model Christian living and let that speak of what Jesus can mean and do in a person's life.

I call the invitation to join the group a sort of 'back door' approach to getting people to see church as a positive force in the community and as a place to relax and enjoy life as well as a place to worship."

Once, when a nonchurch member of the group made negative comments about the church and religion in general, Roy encouraged the person to come on a Sunday and assured him the congregation is not like what he had known. Even if none of the participants come to church, positive things are happening for people in the group. Roy believes that nonchurch people will take up thankful prayer as a result of the fly tying sessions. Roy hopes the group will "continue forever."

Nothing to do with religion?

"We announced the group in the church newsletter and during Sunday worship. We outlined the group's purpose as simply tying flies and, then, kidded a bit by adding we would be 'tying for Jesus.' We were trying to say it was a church-sponsored activity. We were not going to keep God and Christ out of it. It was fellowship. To most people, fly tying has nothing to do with religion. But the session was church sponsored with Jesus present in the spirit. There is no Bible reading or prayer at the sessions, but we keep the session in our prayers and the rector does wear a collar at the sessions.

Knowledge of the group travels by word of mouth. Once during the summer of 1999, two members who belong to Trout Unlimited, a national anglers' organization, demonstrated fly tying at a county fair. They took phone numbers of a dozen or so interested people and invited them to join the group when it started up in the fall. Five of them came."

The present group is intergenerational and averages twelve to fourteen people. Some of the members do not participate in any church. Roy and the rector trust they will come to sense the deeper dimensions of God's presence in every part of life. Roy finds hints of this expectation in the talk that goes beyond laughter and camaraderie. Relaxed and consistent participation over the two years of the group's life has encouraged easy conversation. The young people ask questions and all talk occasionally about church life and about their responsibility for local issues, such as conservation. In all, there is ongoing concern and support for one another in daily living.

What does it mean to the participants? Roy observes, "Most of those who started are still coming and all come eagerly each time. They reflect on daily living in ways people usually do not have time to do. They share things to celebrate and things that cause anxiety, even though talk of pressure in their lives does not come very easily for the adults. Likewise, the youth are stressed but do not show or, even, know it. I believe we have learned not only skills but knowledge about nature, its enjoyment, and its relation to God."

A poor college risk becomes a professor

Roy, a retired education professor, and his wife, Judith, a retired nurse, have raised two daughters and one son. At sixty-three, Roy continues to work part-time as an educational consultant. He travels to southern school systems at risk from high poverty or highly transient children. He helps teachers to use materials and techniques to teach children who need an extra lift. Roy taught literacy education as a professor with the State University of New York.

As a child, Roy became a regular in Sunday School through the home visits of a young evangelical preacher seeking members for his new congregation. The young preacher picked up Roy and some of his brothers and sister in his old car, took them to church, and brought them back home. At age twelve, Roy first glimpsed Jesus' love for him and became a "born-again" Christian. Roy went from high school into the military. The guidance counselor told him that he could not make it in college. Meeting many college-educated people in the service, Roy came to believe that he really could succeed in college and resolved to try.

During his last year in teachers' college, he married. At that time, he had little church involvement and Judith had been participating in a Presbyterian congregation, but with little satisfaction. Judith's Church of England grandmother prevailed on them to seek marriage in the Episcopal Church and to receive the premarital instruction she knew would be offered to them. They both wanted a more spiritual life and they responded readily to the grandmother's desire. They found the pastor young, encouraging, and an enjoyable instructor. The pastor, building the congregation at the time, met with just the two of them for about ten sessions. From that time on, both have been steady participants in the Episcopal Church with their spiritual growth deepening each decade of their thirty-seven years of life together. Growth has occurred through their church activities — through the vestry (the church council of Episcopal congregations) for Roy, through Marriage Encounter (marital enrichment for and led by couples) and Cursillo for both, and through Roy's increased daily Bible reading. Together, they continue the monthly large group meetings of Cursillo.

Roy sees God leading him all the time. He talks about "rough places" — learning how to be married, how to raise children, and how to agree on child rearing practices. Rough times at work were so worrisome that they caused physical illness. Still, both Roy and Judith look forward to each new day.

A teenage glimpse abides

Roy is convinced that God is kind and benevolent. He has an overwhelming sense that God loves him. He sees that love in Jesus who loves him so much he died for him. The intellectual and emotional aspects of that love keep him going. He constantly wonders what, he terms, is "God's plan" for him. Recently, he shared with his minister some near death experiences. Roy asked should he be thankful or wonder why? His minister answered both with a single word, "Yes."

Roy first glimpsed God's love as a teenager. He remembers the peace and security of that love and has looked for a rediscovery of that love ever since. Cursillo a few months ago brought him the closest to revisiting that "born-again" experience of God's love. Hearing other men share their spiritual experiences showed him that they loved God enough to tell others of those experiences. The people supporting the participants in preparing and serving meals and singing to them from hidden places touched him. A bishop was part of the Cursillo. Roy made his first confession to the bishop and valued the penitence suggested by the bishop. All these riches came together during the closing liturgy when Roy sensed, again, an outpouring of the love he had found in his early teens.

Roy tells of connecting his spiritual and his secular life long ago in his daily prayer and ever-growing scripture reading. When he gets up, he prays to be a blessing to someone that day. He finds that, more often than not, he is a blessing to someone. These small efforts bring rewards big enough to keep him going. He summarizes, "I try to live according to what Jesus wants me to do and to be. I do slip. We are all sinners. There is no question my life is better than it would be otherwise — in being caring and just, in being guided when guidance is strongly needed."

Learning to wait

Doing unto others as he would have them do unto him is central for Roy. Central also is prayer to be forgiven for his shortcomings. He tries hard to forgive others for theirs. He is guided the most by asking, "What would Jesus do?" He comments, "Often, I do not know the answer, so I take my best shot. At other times, I see clearly what Jesus would do or not do. I strive to be just and honest. I fail often, but I keep trying. I hope that, in my lapses, no one gets harmed. I do not want to cause anyone grief — whether loved ones or strangers. I'd rather suffer pain myself than give it to someone else."

In his professional life, Roy tries to make the educational system more just where it is unjust. At times, this has cost him immensely — to the point of the physical illness noted. He continues in that struggle. He finds that God has made the road easier in retirement. He does not seem to have to fight as hard. He senses God saying, "Someone else can carry on that fight, Roy." He works for change more easily now. He has learned to apply principles of change gradually and wait for the change he seeks to evolve.

Roy still recalls teachers from elementary school through college, friends, and relatives who made a difference in his life. He sees them as blessings on his path to "being closer and closer to Jesus and God." For his first twenty to thirty years, he says, "I was not aware I was traveling a path. Now in my sixties, I am convinced I was on a path. Jesus was there leading me even though I was not aware of him and not loving him as much as I do now. There is no way I could have gotten through those things without him." He comments further, "I have a philosophy that has only now come to me: Humanity could never exist without God's grace. The more I understand about my fellow human beings and the world and its functioning — the more I see the weakness of humanity — the more I am convinced that we exist by God's grace alone. Things that could not possibly be remedied by mankind still get better. That improvement comes only by God's grace." ✦

Chapter 7 — In the Church

Mary Ann: A Mission in a Vacation Bible School

Working with children in a church program calls for flexibility, skill, and commitment. When the Vacation Bible School was challenged to address the needs of the children more directly, Mary Ann adapted the curriculum to their needs.

A needed curriculum change

St. Luke's and All Saints Episcopal Church is an urban church in densely populated northern New Jersey; the congregation of a handful is served by an Anglo supply priest. The neighborhood is now predominantly Chinese-American. Five years ago under the leadership of a part-time Chinese priest, the congregation started a nine-week, full-day Bible School and activity program for children in the neighborhood. For the first three years, the primary goal was community service and income. Bible stories were taught only as history for two hours per week. The fourth year, Mary Ann took over and expanded the length and depth of the teaching. Each child received six hours per week of biblical teaching with the explicit intention of introducing the children to Jesus Christ as one to trust, to ask for help, and to try to follow in their daily living.

Mary Ann relates, "Only a very few of the children had ever gone to a church anywhere. Many of the parents were sending their children simply for the day care. By this fourth year, we felt free to be more explicitly Christian than in previous years. We believed it was time to help the children to come to know something of God in Jesus Christ and the Old Testament background for him. We knew there would be no help from home. We also knew the children would tell their parents what happened each day and that the parents would listen to what the children wanted to tell. Thus, the parents would receive a kind of 'low-key' introduction to Jesus Christ."

The school itself met daily from 9:00 a.m. to 5:00 p.m. for nine weeks. Some children came as early as 8:30 and some stayed until 5:30. Mary Ann led the staff as a certified teacher, assisted by volunteers of whom three were college students and two were high school seniors. Mary Ann and one of the college students came from St. Luke's and All Saints. The others came from a nearby Pentecostal congregation. Twenty-five to thirty children came daily. They were divided into three groups by age. A Bible story session with Mary Ann, a session with the team from the other church, and a play period filled the morning. Music and dance and games filled the afternoon. The music and dance time were spent preparing to present an hour-long version of *Godspell* at the end of the nine weeks. Thus, the participants worked with biblical material in the afternoon as well.

"As we set to work, relationship concerns arose in the youngest group. An eight-year-old girl who spoke little English became quite frustrated with not understanding what was going on around her. When the others excluded her, she tried to force her way in. In her frustration, she began to yell and to hit others. Also, a six-year-old boy seemed to play by himself most of the time. When others tried to join him, he appeared to want them to do everything his way. We could not be sure just what was happening. Perhaps, he had high inclusion needs and, when he was not invited in, he just stayed out. Apparently, he had not yet developed the social skills for such occasions. Moreover, this boy and girl often came into conflict with each other. Incidentally, they were in the same Bible group because the girl's parents requested she be in the younger group. The parents had thought she would find the work easier because of her limited English.

We were not prepared to deal with all we were encountering. First, I tried to change the two children's behavior. I soon realized that was inappropriate. I needed to help all of the other twenty-five to thirty children to work together better. We had to change the curriculum to address this situation. We began to teach principles of how to act with one another as the curriculum.

At that point, I believe God led me to find and borrow from another congregation the videotaped puppets of *Quigley's Village* (from Cornerstone Video, TVA/Television Associates, Inc., 2410 Charleston Road, Mountain View, CA 94043 for Zondervan Publishing House). Prepared for ages two to seven, they presented themes such as 'Responsibility,' 'Working Things Out,' and 'Cooperation.' We tied the videos into the printed materials from the David C. Cook curriculum for Sundays. Those materials did not make sense until paired with the videotapes. We could relate the story of a biblical figure's actions to similar situations the children faced. We worked a story for two days, and we found that the contemporary stories and the art work from the Cook material worked well together."

Putting everyone on the team

"My son, Peter, served as a leader for the activities of arts, crafts, and games. Talking through the situation with him and my proposal for what to do was enough to draw him in. I talked with the whole team about ways to teach children how much Jesus loves them all in spite of their actions. Since Jesus forgives us when we do wrong, we can learn to forgive each other in the same way. With the children, I talked about needing to think, talk, and act in love, not hate, in care, not cruelty. These are the ways God wants us to live all the time, not just when we talk about a person in the Bible.

A church member asked if there had been many conversions. I answered that I really believe that I could say, 'Yes.' I believe many of the children left us feeling that they truly had a friend in Jesus to whom they could turn whenever they wanted. I believe these children became better instruments of reconciliation, justice, and love. Further, I even believe that, given the opportunity, many of them would try to come to church on a regular basis."

Harmony

"I used *Quigley's Village* videos in the Bible time with this youngest group. The tapes illustrated learning about friendship; forgiveness; love; and anger. Bible stories reflecting these issues combined with Cook's puppet stories of everyday events helped the children to see what happened when people acted inappropriately. Then we looked at our living together here and now.

Relationships among all of the children began to improve. In particular, the boy had begun to want to be with others more than to be alone. The girl was building close relationships with some of the other girls. At times, I still had to intervene in fights and use 'time-outs' but not with the frequency of the early summer.

In the older Bible groups, we studied the same principles but without Mr. Quigley and his village. Both teams centered on how much Jesus loves children all the time — even times when they do things wrong. As Jesus forgives us when we do wrong, we need to learn to forgive each other in the same way. Even God was talked about freely! And, we talked about the experiences of a few who had gone to church and what children and youth can do as part of worship.

Aided by the employment of a young woman with theatrical talents, the performance of *Godspell* went well. The parents loved it. The whole program made an impact on the parents. The children told them each day's story and what they wanted to share about it. They also brought home daily handouts. I believe the parents continued to send their kids every day because more was going on than just good day care.

This time, I felt a lot more positive about what we had taught, the way we had taught it, and what the children had learned. You might say we became just a bit more aware of cultural diversity, too."

Mary Ann searches, lapses, and returns

Mary Ann and her husband, Robert, have three of their four sons still living at home. Mary Ann has severe arthritis, needs hip and knee replacements, and is applying for disability funds. Before surgery is possible, she must cope with a serious weight problem. While no longer able to work as a substitute teacher, she is able to work as a poll inspector for elections. Robert keeps the books for a small investment company and does most of the housework. He commutes fifty miles each way because a job change would end insurance coverage for Mary Ann. Of the sons: John works in home construction; Daniel manages an insurance claims section; and Peter, a sophomore in college, is working for an associate's degree in criminal justice and wants to pass the tests that qualify him as a forest ranger. The sons contribute to home expenses and upkeep as their means and skills allow. The oldest son, Eric, is married and lives within an hour's drive.

Mary Ann describes her parents as "Christmas and Easter" people. "Dragged" to Sunday School as a child, she then helped to teach as a teenager, Mary Ann always felt something was missing and not right. Once married, she worshiped only occasionally. Her congregation began to decline in the familiar pattern of inner city congregations. For the past decade, the church has alternated between part-time and Sunday supply clergy. At the present, the church is requesting diocesan aid.

In the early eighties, Mary Ann became relatively disaffected with her church because of some decisions by the church council about a previous clergy-person. In 1985, she had a religious experience that led her back to intensive worship. She was searching to know what had happened to her and to know more about God. Her intense participation continues to this day. She has become the congregation's volunteer secretary, a position she carries on in spite of her disability. A sense of call led her to work for and to complete a Master of Divinity degree as a part-time student from 1991 to 1998. Substitute teaching filled the rest of her work time and, for four years, she has run the church's Vacation Bible School.

Light in the dark

Mary Ann's faith came to life through her religious experience of October 1985. Times were difficult that year. She had broken her foot, her health was bad, money was short, and her mother was in the hospital with cancer. Unhappy with her congregation as well, she "felt like God was giving up" on her. A Pentecostal friend from Florida came to visit. During a hospital visit to her mother, the friend invited Mary Ann to come forward to join in prayer for her mother. Recalling the moment, she says, "I joined them even though I did not want to. At that point, I felt like I was on fire, all the room blanked out, and there was a white light that got brighter and brighter. It was fantastic. That bright light was opposed to the darkness that had been so much a part of my life. Later, my friend told me I had been born again. I let Jesus into my life and I ran to God after that." Her pastor helped her through the experience as she took up worshiping three times a week and daily Bible reading. He said, "God got tired of waiting for you so He hit you over the head with a bolt of lightning." Of her seminary experience, Mary Ann reflects, "I went because I felt God was telling me to go. I have had voices in my life at prayer time.

In 1985, I started connecting my faith and my living. I now connect what I read in the Bible with life," she says. "Learning to preach, I learned to connect things from life today with the Bible. When someone has a problem, I ask how did Jesus deal with that sort of thing. Then, how can I deal with that. Often, I see things that lead me to say, 'I suspect maybe this is why things are happening for you as they do.'

I find that if I do not take the time for God each day, I have a problem," Mary Ann says. "I pray for God to help me and show me the light and the right way to go in daily life. I know that as much as I hurt, God is not doing this to me. God is with me and God loves me and will not do anything to hurt me. I just have to be patient and things will eventually go right in God's time. I believe that totally. That has brought me through the past fifteen years," Mary Ann believes.

A more fervent ethic

Mary Ann is succinct and pointed: "Love God. Love family. Don't hurt people. If you do, go back and ask them to forgive you. I hope other people can find God through me. I do not believe all of us need to be hit over the head as I was. Others do better with some type of slowly growing insight. I learned these basics through my family, my friends, and the times I was in church. However, it took that experience in 1985 to make them the intense part of my life that they are today." ✦

Robbie: A Mission to Develop Indian Youths as Church Leaders

Young people need training to become leaders in the church. Seeing the potential among the participants at a church conference for Indian youths, Robbie and five others on the leadership team decided to work with the young people to develop their leadership skills. They believed all of them would, thereby, be strengthened in their walk with Christ. The six chose "Strong Heart Ministries" as the name for their new direction.

Proud of something

"The work I have done in the Episcopal Church has provided me with joy. I have always wanted to share these feelings with others and to have them experience, with me, Christ's love. Many youths during their teens and early adulthood are continuously searching for a comfortable place. At that age, they are not quite sure what it is that can bring such rewards. But they are hoping they will find that certain pleasure that makes them feel safe and comfortable. It seems that 'feeling at home' comes when they are with other youths who share their Native American history and their Episcopal background and are surrounded by the warm acceptance of their Indian elders.

Many times I have contemplated what is it, exactly, that the Lord is calling me to do within the Episcopal Church. While I continue to listen for his word, I do know that I have always been called to work with the young and help them recognize the love of Jesus Christ. I believe that many people go through the motions of being an Episcopalian. Churches need a spiritual reawakening; members have become bored from the repetition. Often, Sunday worship becomes routine.

Many of the young people I know are not outspoken and are reluctant to share their feelings for Christ with others. Youths from other communions seem ready to share their convictions about Christianity and their faith. I believe that, for our youths to move forward, we have to share our feelings. If we see others having a great time and enjoying their faith and it is all right to do so, we will begin to do it too. Being proud of their faith will help them to become more focused and grounded. A lot of youths go through challenging times today — alcohol and drug abuse and gangs are on the rise on reservations. Becoming proud of something and standing up for what you believe in will help other youths to stand strong."

Both Indian and Christian

"Churches need to be reawakened to what they were founded for. Members need to be more involved in their congregations and know they are there for Christ and for the Gospel. We need to reflect on the week's Gospel and our daily living much more. We need clergy to be more actively involved in the daily lives of their congregations. Congregations need to discover ways to keep young people interested in the church. More youth events need to be held locally, in deaneries, dioceses, and provinces. We need to bring youths together to discuss the issues of alcohol and drug abuse, gangs, unemployment, and poverty. When you are poor, it is hard to conceive of another way of living. Young people need to talk about the things that affect them and to develop solutions that will work.

Many Native youths have difficulty relating their Indian tradition and culture to the Episcopal tradition. Young people feel they have been told by others that these traditional beliefs are wrong or that the two can't be mixed. In fact, certain ceremonies and dances have been described as 'not proper!' Youths need to be shown how it is all right to believe in their own traditions. They need to be provided with the tools to compare both the differences and the similarities between Native American belief systems and Christian belief systems. For example, for the Paiutes, the water from their lake is very sacred to them and they use the water in their worship. We need to show youths the linkages between water in their tradition and water in the Christian tradition.

I will continue to support the youth ministries of the Episcopal Church. I will advocate for youths at the local and national levels. I will continue to work to empower and challenge the youths to develop ministry with young people within their congregations.

I want to see more Indian youths become more involved with the Episcopal Church, to be proud of who and what they are as Indians, as Christians, and as Episcopalians. I will work to encourage the acceptance of tribal traditions and culture in the church. I am part of a move in this direction that took shape at a Native American Episcopal Youth Event. Since our Native American young face a lot and need to be strong in their daily struggles, we chose the name 'Strong Heart Ministries' for this work. Through Strong Heart Ministries, we want to find effective ways to work with the youths and, for all of us, to become stronger in our walk with Christ."

Open to challenge

"We want to make 'Strong Heart' evangelical in the spirit of our Gospel Based Discipleship. [In this method of Bible study, a Gospel passage is read three times. Participants move from sharing what catches their attention to what Jesus is saying to each of them to what Jesus is asking each of them to do.] We want to present God and the feelings of spirituality within the group. As we work, we believe God is leading us to raise up future leaders with a Christian knowledge and foundation for the Episcopal Church.

I let people know I am part of the Episcopal Church and that opens the conversation. I talk about what I do and why I enjoy it so much. I try to get people to go to church with me. I talk about the liturgy and sermons and how much I enjoy them. When I read the Book of Common Prayer, I find the language very rich and rewarding. I enjoy the approach Indian Ministries has taken in developing their own prayers reflecting the strong faith of Native American peoples. I talk about the Episcopal Church as a teaching church and its openness to the challenge of people offering their own interpretations.

When I encourage people to be part of the Episcopal Church, I talk about communion's strong function. I share that, for me, when I take communion, things are cleared for me and I talk about the time after communion when I kneel and pray and thank God for all God has offered me.

Recently, I took two friends to church with me — one was raised as a Mormon and the other as a Pentecostal. We talked about the one cup. I said, 'In the common cup, Jesus is, symbolically, sharing his cup with us.' I explained that when we go through the scripture of ' . . . take, eat, and drink . . . ,' I feel I am actually drinking from and eating from his hand."

Worth the effort

Robbie finds that when he talks about "Strong Heart Ministries" there is positive response. He finds that Native youths respond well. He expects it will be challenging to recruit them for leadership training, but worth the effort.

Robbie comments, "So often, there is no one else to talk to about the Lord Jesus Christ and what He means to us as Native peoples." Some of his nonchurch friends recall the negative impact white Christianity has had on Indians. But, they like what Robbie says about the Episcopal Church. One of them recently asked to visit his church to see what it is like.

The six of us will meet soon in Minneapolis to set goals and objectives. We may meet with the Rev. Doyle Turner of the Indian Theological Training Institute. If we find that ITTI may be educational for the young people, we will schedule Doyle for presentations. We plan to use the next Native American Episcopal Youth Event to bring more people into 'Strong Heart Ministries.'"

From sub to the first team

Robbie, in his early thirties, is single and lives in Falls Church, Virginia. He is a member of the Poarch Band of Creek Indians. He works as a special assistant to the Office of American Indian Trusts (OAIT) in Washington, D.C. He carries out initiatives specified by the director of OAIT and of the Assistant Secretary of Indian Affairs. He has worked on a consultation policy reflecting the former President's Executive Order to mandate federal agencies to consult with tribal leaders about policies affecting Indian people as policies are developed. He also serves on the advisory committee for the Native youth event that is sponsored by the Bureau of Indian Affairs.

When asked about his faith, Robbie spoke candidly. "I am still young and still trying to find my way. I am having a blast. I believe in good works. Also, I know we walk by grace alone. I enjoy reading Christian writing — both interpretation and fiction. Lately, I find myself listening to a Christian radio station every morning. I look up the passage being discussed to understand what the caller or speaker is talking about. In the next year, I want to get more involved in the daily living of my faith."

His father had been at a Catholic seminary until he was called into the service for Viet Nam. During his early years, Robbie went to the Catholic church with his family. He recalls his father having a strong faith. The family — Robbie, his parents, and his younger brother — moved to Poarch, Alabama, about sixty miles north of Mobile, when he was sixteen. His parents let him choose where he wanted to go to church. He often went where his friends went. He began going to St. Anna's Episcopal Church in Poarch and joined its youth group. The Poarch Band of Creek Indians makes up the community and the congregation of St. Anna's. The priest and his wife were a strong influence on Robbie during his late teens and early twenties.

When Robbie was twenty, he went to a Paths Crossing in Pine Ridge, South Dakota. [Paths Crossing is an annual gathering of members of Native and Anglo Episcopal congregations for dialogue and mutual support.] His mother was asked to represent their congregation but, since she did not want to travel alone, Robbie was asked to go in her place. There, he met Native spiritual leaders in the Episcopal Church. They invited him to participate in national level work with them. This participation has become an important part of his life and commitment.

When he was twenty-two and armed with a college degree in anthropology, Robbie returned to Poarch as a social worker. He provided intensive case management to victims of abuse and neglect and to their families on the reservation. He also worked with youths and their families involved in the court system, offering parenting classes and cultural activities for the young. Enjoying the work and helping his people, he continued his education at the University of Alabama earning a bachelor's degree in social work. During courses at UA, he worked in residential treatment with adolescent boys who suffered from emotional and psychological disorders and were involved in the court systems. A scholarship for a master's degree in social work took him to George Washington University in St. Louis. During graduate school, he continued his work in residential treatment. Dr. Eddie Brown, the director of the Buder Center for American Indian Studies at the university and, previously, the Assistant Secretary for Indian Affairs at the Department of the Interior, thought every student should have a Washington, D.C. experience. At his suggestion, after graduation, Robbie moved to Washington and went to work as a program analyst at the Bureau of Indian Affairs.

At present, Robbie's congregational involvement is limited to Sunday worship in the church near his home in Falls Church. As far as he knows, there are no other Native Episcopalians in the area. He is the only Indian in the congregation. His friends in the Washington area are mostly Native American professionals who work in national Indian affairs. He is exploring ordination and church conferences add to his developing faith. He wants to take an evening course at nearby Virginia Theological Seminary to keep growing spiritually.

Support for faithful living

What counts for Robbie is being a good person by listening to others and offering advice when it is asked for. "I often find myself defending a lot of people to others; this is not always healthy. With my background in social work, I have learned to look at a situation in various ways, before offering a suggestion. I try to treat everyone equally. I am not afraid to talk about my church involvement. Washington has a young, professional society where we are all about politics and making a difference."

Robbie learned these principles and how to live them from his parents. He recalls he always wanted to make them proud of him and not disappoint them. He resisted drugs and alcohol in high school. He didn't let anything affect his grades or his relationship with his parents. He continues his growth in living his principles through phone calls with his parents several times a week. He talks even more with his brother — married and the father of two — whom he finds strong and wise in living as a Christian. ✦

Missions of Groups Within the Congregation

Congregations abound with small groups. Some are task groups such as vestries, altar guilds, and buildings and grounds and worship committees. Others are devoted to learning the faith such as classes for children and discussion groups for adults following worship. Some groups focus on fellowship altogether. Still others are support groups for daily living such as small groups that meet regularly for biblical reflection.

The life of each of these groups can provide rich experiences in personal transformation and in preparation for life Monday to Saturday. In all aspects of their life, all of these groups need to be caring, fair, and prayerful. Their maintenance and oversight are a genuine field of mission. Both leaders and members do well to consult the legions of resources available to assess and to enhance the quality of the group life in their congregation. Many say that they learned to work with other people in their church life. Deeper still, many say their primary religious insights and experiences came in the midst of their church groups.

Too many times, however, maintenance and oversight of these groups can consume all of the available time and energy of both leaders and members. There is very little vision and energy left for groups to be formed around missions beyond the congregation. Too many congregations point to providing their buildings as meeting places for nonchurch groups as their only community service. Still more serious is the failure of congregations to have vision and energy left to support each of their members in their daily living. When these things happen, maintenance has usurped mission. It is time for congregations to begin to focus on supporting their members in each of the mission fields described in the preceding stories. ✦

Missions of Groups
Beyond the Congregation

The effective missions of individuals do not negate or replace the more familiar congregational missions of committees and task forces carried on beyond the congregation and in its name. Such missions serve people in need through a food shelf, a shelter for battered women and families, a counseling service, or the like. Other missions work to correct injustice in the local or wider society by sponsoring computer training for unskilled people or setting up new procedures for juvenile justice. Other missions work for environmental responsibility. Others work for peace within and between nations. Many times, several congregations work together on these tasks. Regional bodies of denominations often partner to influence social policy as in Lloyd's story of resistance to the lottery in Wisconsin. In the United States, the role of the churches collaborating in the struggle for civil rights is probably their greatest work of mission as a body in the past century. Whole worldwide communions join together in the World Council of Churches, which links all three concerns in its program of Justice, Peace, and the Integrity of Creation.

These missions are familiar ones. Church publications carry their stories already. They do not need recounting here. Do not miss their absolute necessity in both local and wider settings. As a body, the church must be seen as a compassionate friend of the needy and an advocate for justice for the weak. Given human greed and lust for power, every relief of one hurt or injustice is followed by some new abuse calling for correction. The struggle against evil is ongoing.

Vigilant congregations lead and train their members to evangelize through these missions. Members point to God's work in Jesus Christ as the reason they talk and act as they do. They offer the worship and community of the church as the place to find direction and power. The word and sacrament of Jesus' table offer personal transformation. As nonchurch people investigate Christian worship and congregational life, they begin to find themselves transformed and begin to become agents of Jesus' reign.

The words of Christians have the greatest impact when they are preceded by actions that meet human need and call for the correction of injustice. The civil rights movement brought evangelizing moments because deeds in the struggle for justice gave authenticity to words about Jesus Christ as leader and helper, as Lord and Savior. Food shelves organized by churches are correct to include invitations to Sunday worship with the food they distribute. Missions beyond the church are old, not new, ways to "call people to faith." Costly deeds present Jesus Christ.

These missions are familiar and expected. However, too often, vision for mission does not see beyond them. Missionary spirituality affirms these missions while it goes beyond them to the, often, more transforming missions of individual members. Eddie calls for his law firm to change the way it deals with mistakes. Susan leads her community to house its people caringly and justly. They do the kinds of things that food shelves, resolutions, and demonstrations often cannot do. ✦

PART TWO

Organizing a Congregation Around
the Members as the Missionaries

*". . . like a man building a house, who dug deeply
and laid the foundation on rock." (Luke 6:48)*

INTRODUCTION: PART TWO

Part One introduced the vision of the members as missionaries and the stories of fifteen missionaries. Part Two introduces a way to reorganize a congregation around this vision in these steps:

1. Clarifying your own sense of the vision
   Chapter 8 — Getting Your Head and Heart into the Vision

2. Sharpening your own vision and forming a team
   Chapter 9 — We Need "Hubble-eyes." Preparation and Team Formation

3. Redesigning the congregation
   Chapter 10 — Let's Redesign

4. Providing a guide for decision making by the missionaries
   Chapter 11 — Decision Making for the Missionaries

5. Developing a spirituality that works for missionaries
   Chapter 12 — Missionary Spirituality: The Kind that Supports Missionaries

6. Orienting seekers as missionaries
   Chapter 13 — Helping People to Become Missionaries

7. Looking at some ways missionaries make changes
   Chapter 14 — Change Agents at Work

8. Providing support for missionaries in ongoing small groups
   Chapter 15 — Some Specifics About Small Groups

9. Planning worship and preaching that nurture missionaries
   Chapter 16 — How Worship and Preaching Can Nurture the Vision

10. Developing the leadership style and skills the vision needs
    Chapter 17 — The Kind of Leaders This Vision Needs

Chapter 8 — Getting Your Head and Heart into the Vision

This vision of the laity as today's primary missionaries challenges assumptions. Here are issues to face as you work toward a vision of the members as the missionaries. Work through them alone or with others. And, pray for guidance as you consider each one.

The mission has the church as its visible instrument

The church is the visible instrument of the mission of God in Jesus Christ. We err to say the church has a mission. Rather, the mission has a church. The key insight is that mission is the mission of God. God sends. God sends Jesus and the church shares in Jesus' being sent, Jesus' mission. Always, the mission is God's mission.

Explore this issue further in its more conventional theological term of *missio Dei*. In *Transforming Mission: Paradigm Shifts in the Theology of Mission* (Orbis, 1991) David J. Bosch reviews the biblical and historical background of mission and the Roman Catholic and Orthodox practice of it. He sees *missio Dei* as the moment of a paradigm shift from the modern to the post-modern era. He sees today's many modes of mission as the "emerging ecumenical paradigm" by which all communions participate in mission.

This is revolutionary for many Christians. In the Episcopal *Book of Common Prayer*, "mission" appears in the "The Church" section of "An Outline of the Faith," p. 855. No wonder we have to work to become "mission-minded." In 1835, Episcopal leaders chose The Domestic and Foreign Missionary Society of the Protestant Episcopal Church as their corporate name. As noted earlier, they were more than a hundred years ahead of their time in beginning with mission, not membership. The result of the Christian mission cannot be to bring to people into the church. The end has to be the building up of the world by those baptized in Jesus Christ who live as agents of the reign of God — as missionaries.

My colleague, Jim Anderson, who is also on the Executive Committee of the Alumni/ae Association of the Virginia Theological Seminary, told me about a discussion there — whether students were being prepared to take their honored and proper role in the institution of the church or to be in the world as missionaries. The committee reaffirmed that the Seminary's goal was to train missionaries for today's world where the mission is at the door of the church. The two of us went on to talk about the laity being missionaries as well. He, wryly, observed that the culture of the church has made and continues to make the church an end in itself. The Seminary's graduates swim against a strong tide when they try to train the laity to be missionaries in the world.

I had first encountered this question in practice while serving as the ordained leader of a congregation in the mid sixties. I came across the study of "The Structure of the Missionary Congregation," which had been commissioned by the Third Assembly of the World Council of Churches at New Delhi in 1961. The study was carried on by the Department of Studies in Evangelism. I also encountered the work of the Department of the Laity of the WCC and its periodical, *Laity*. I was part of the Department of the Laity's consultation on "Human Engineering and Christian Growth" in Bossey, Switzerland, in 1965. At its end, I toured the Lay Academies of Germany (see *Church and World Encounter*, Lee J. Gable, United Church Press, 1964). Helmut Thielicke and Eberhard Mueller had organized them after World War II to influence the rebuilding of Germany along Christian lines. During my service as rector of St. Paul's, Montvale, New Jersey, Eberhard Mueller helped me to organize a local expression of their method, known as The Pascack Valley Center (PVC). It was an interfaith community ministry. (For a report on the PVC, go to www.rylib-web.man.ac.uk, web site of the John Rylands University Library. In its Special Collection Guide, go to the Audenshaw Foundation Archive, and find "The Pascack Valley Center, A Shared Experience in Community Ministry," Audenshaw Document No. 33, April, 1974.) However, the WCC study, the lay academies, and the small Pascack Valley Center were all works of the church as a body. Along the way, I met Mark Gibbs, consultant, author, and, at the time, head of the association of European lay training centers. He introduced me to the concept of daily mission fields. That introduction started my ongoing reflection on the missions of individual Christians in their daily arenas.

Today's primary missionaries: the laity

Usually, we think of mission as "what the church does in the world." When we say "church," we usually mean the congregation or some larger church body. We don't think about what the individual members "do in the world" as mission. It is time to see what individual Christians do as mission. When we do, we take a giant step from the past into a new reality of mission.

The "mainline" denominations have been "sidelined." Today, religious leaders center on the private concerns of the family and on individualistic spirituality. The church and its leaders are no longer found where the crucial decisions of social, economic, and political policy are made. While the church as an institution is not usually present where key decisions are made, its members are.

Two contemporary "parables" tell the story. The first concerns control of chlorofluorocarbons or "CFCs," which are used in refrigeration. CFCs deplete the ozone layer, which protects all life from too much sun. One company in the United States controlled 85 percent of the CFCs in the world. The head of the company accepted the request of the U. S. government to stop making CFCs. The project was turned over to two executives, both Episcopalians. They completed the dismantling of all CFC production ahead of schedule. They believed in the project. Perhaps, they found support for their diligence in the resolutions of church councils calling for the end of CFC production. Indispensable was the work of these two Christians who were in the right place at the right time. Resolutions alone could not have ended the dismantling.

The other "parable" is suggested by our proverb — "the hand that rocks the cradle rocks the world." While referring to mothers, it expresses the impact of early conditioning on each one of us. The primary missionaries in the home are not the clergy, vestry / church council, or congregation, but the parents or their stand-ins. Suppose one of those parents is a Christian. We trust she or he connects child care and nurturing with God's call to be loving and fair and to teach love and fairness. We trust he or she makes known his or her own ultimate commitments and encourages both spouse and children to explore and, perhaps, to find their own place at Jesus' table to be fed.

Mission moves through a certain progression for the individual Christian. First come loving and just actions. Then come words that interpret the actions. Finally, when appropriate, come invitations to explore the Christian way.

A professor at a state teachers' college showed unusual readiness to help students in difficulty. When some students praised her, she said, "I believe helping students is part of teaching." She had already made her Christian commitment known through pictures in her office of the church youth group she led. Accordingly, her students understood her "belief" to be explicitly Christian, rather than only philosophical. Those same pictures encouraged students to ask her about nearby churches as they found their own religious quest surfacing.

The Honorable Byron Rushing, as 9th Suffolk District Representative to the Massachusetts State Legislature, talked about his mission there at a conference on December 1, 1992. "The ministry of making Christ known and renewing the world is the ministry of all the baptized — an extraordinary calling for ordinary people. I am always amazed when other Christians say how difficult it must be for me to be a practicing Christian, while working within a system that is perceived to be self-serving, corrupt, and ruthless. My first reaction is to reply as a legislator: 'No, I don't think my colleagues are any more corrupt, or any more virtuous, for that matter, than the workers in most other institutions: banks, hospitals, computer firms, churches.'"

Rushing continues, "The government is like any other part of the world: It is fallen and unreconciled. And that is why it is an opportunity for me. It ultimately belongs to Christ, and I am called to share in renewing it. I am in the legislature because Jesus is in the legislature, and I am in the legislature because I am called to follow Jesus. You are in the insurance business because Jesus is in the insurance business, and you are called to follow Jesus. If Jesus is not there, don't bother. You shouldn't be there, either.

An elected official is expected to have a special concern for the people who live in his or her district. In baptism, we all inherit a constituency. It is everybody else. We are called to a special relationship with God's world, striving for justice among all people and respecting the dignity of every human being," Rushing aptly concludes.

The mission of each Christian is, then, to bring to every arena of daily life, in deed and word, the good news of God's work in Jesus Christ. These arenas include our daily work, our homes, our local communities, the wider world (of society, culture, economics, and government), our leisure time, and our faith community. In more traditional language, the mission is to proclaim and work, in deed and word, for the reign of God in all human life and the creation.

Reorganizing the congregation around the daily missions of the members

The average congregation is not organized around the daily missions of its members. Maintenance is constantly emphasized over mission. We need to go further. Ezra Earl Jones, recently retired General Secretary, Board of Discipleship, United Methodist Church, uses secular organizational development theory to take us the next step in seeing the church as a system and asking what it produces. The church is not producing members who are missionaries. The church is producing "compliant, loyal members" — a phrase coined by Jim Anderson, an ordained minister as well as a systems consultant — who believe that they have just three duties: go to church every Sunday; work toward the tithe; and do what the clergy tell them. To change what the system produces, the system has to change. Without changing the system, you continue to get what you have always gotten. What counts, then, is your resolve as a leader to change the system!

As leader and change agent you must note these insights from organizational development theory (the following is an adaptation of Jones's view):

- If you keep doing what you have always done, you will get what you have always gotten. The system is designed for the results it is getting.

- If you want different results, improve or change the system. If a system is continually improved, year by year, in ten years you begin to achieve what you want.

- If you want different results, be clear about the different results you want; design the system to give those results; and manage the system to produce those results.

- Manage the system to produce the desired results, beginning at the top and permeating the whole system (organization). This means everyone at every level takes responsibility to manage the change at his or her level.

Beginning to change a system takes a decade. Ten years can seem a long time. Angus Dun, a former bishop of Washington, D. C., used to say, "It is hard to be patient with the terrible patience of God." When you set aside the culture's demand for a quick fix, there is good news: Hang in there for ten years and you will begin to see substantive changes in the congregation — changes from self-concern to concern for the daily missions of its members.

George L. Peabody, a Washington, D. C. consultant to secular and church systems (gpeabo@aol.com), observes that this reorganization is really a paradigm shift; a shift from an existing paradigm of the congregation as a kind of corporate missionary to a new paradigm of each member as a missionary. He comments, "Changing or shifting a paradigm is ten times more difficult than normal social change." Jerry B. Harvey in *How Come Every Time I Get Stabbed in the Back, My Fingerprints Are on the Knife* (Jossey-Bass, 1999), a professor of management science at George Washington University in Washington, D.C., analyzes why it is so difficult. He says we are wrong to talk of "resistance to change." When change means losing a belief system we have leaned on or depended on, we go into a psychological depression. We are not resisting change. We are resisting the loss of a belief system on which we have depended. To move from being compliant, loyal members to being active agents of change for Jesus Christ is to lose a belief system on which we have depended. Leaders can expect strong resistance to such a loss. It is resistance to loss, not to change. (For more on paradigms and their shift, see Appendix B.)

Take heart to persevere from the words of the Archbishop of Canterbury, George L. Carey, on his first visit to the United States in 1992:

> "Christ came to bring us a kingdom, not a church. The church, precious as it undoubtedly is, has been and must always be a vehicle of mission to the world, so that many may be initiated and come into the kingdom. The revolution I am proposing would call for a suspension of all normal church activities to enable a start from a wholly new perspective. The church must now become concerned with both strategy and enabling in a way that responds directly to the 'front-line' needs of its lay members.

> If we accept that God has put each of us in a certain place — be it a factory, boardroom, home, college, community, world — then that is the place where we are called to exercise a royal priesthood as Christians in the world. The local church and its structures must come second to the needs of those serving Christ in the world and the real needs of the communities in which we live."

Worship and Christian community — heartland and homeland of the missionaries

Being on mission every moment is wearing. Missionaries need help to find their directions and to follow them. The "heartland" of a nation is the region where its main strengths are found. Here, in strength, are its agriculture, its industry, its education, its economy, and its governance. Where is the heartland of the missionaries? Worship, corporate and individual, is the heartland of the Christian nation. Individual worship is rooted in corporate worship. Corporate worship is rooted in the word and the sacrament. Here are the symbols and the actions that express their daily living. Through the Holy Spirit, the word read and spoken gives direction for what is to be done in Christ's name "out there." Out there, they will strain to hear the words of love and justice saying this is the path, not that one. The bread and the wine satisfy the hunger and thirst for power to live out the directions coming through the word. Receiving the bread and the cup, they receive the power that feeds them every moment out there. Worship is not the means to the end of mission. It is the heartland of the mission; the place of direction and power to follow it.

To be on mission every moment is to be vulnerable every moment. Home is a place of safety and love. The Christian community is the home of the missionaries. Here one knows others and is known. Here one loves others and is loved. Family size groups of three to six or eight can, even better, provide the knowing and the loving that make for being "home." In small groups, the baptized are guided and supported as they discover and take on their mission fields. In small groups, each continues to share how her or his missions are going. Here each continues to receive the support of encouragement, suggestion, and prayer from one's own people. Wherever we are during the week the community is there too. We are one in the Spirit, regardless of the miles separating us. We can do what we do in our mission fields because our eyes of faith see "a cloud of witnesses" surrounding and supporting us.

If you don't have these qualities in your congregation, remember that no congregation is perfect. Lucifer's favorite workstation is the church. Yet, in spite of all its shortfalls, Jesus' table and Jesus' people are a miracle. Think over your life and the place of Jesus' table and Jesus' people in it. Have you not somehow, somewhere received an everlasting sense of direction and power to follow it from Jesus' table and Jesus' people? Jesus' table and Jesus' people are a miracle. ✦

Chapter 9 — We Need "Hubble-eyes": Preparation and Team Formation

Where do you look for people on mission?

Where do you look when you want to find people on mission? We need "Hubble-eyes" like the telescope that sees as far as it possibly can. We should want to see all the way from Monday to Saturday in each member's life. Most of the time, our eyes work like radar. When our sight hits the "walls" of the church, it bounces back without looking any further. "Hubble-vision" sees missions that "radar-vision" does not even suspect are out there. Can you see the missionaries in their daily arenas? Figure 1 illustrates what "Hubble-vision" sees.

How do you measure your congregation's effectiveness in mission? True missionary effectiveness is unknown until you begin to look at the living of each member in each of his or her daily arenas. How do you do that? I have found it takes at least two hour-long sessions. The questions are easy. "Tell me something of your life at/in (one of the six daily arenas) and what you find yourself doing to make it better." Be prepared for the time and listening energy it takes to hear the answers accurately. Learn by asking twelve people this year.

"Member-missions" and "body-missions"

The inability to see the missions of the members is due to focus on "body-missions alone." "Bodymissions" have long been the only form of missions a congregation can recognize. "Bodymissions" are missions undertaken by a committee of the congregation or by the congregation as a whole. A food shelf and a refugee resettlement undertaken by a committee or task group of a congregation are "body-missions." In the Missionary Spirituality Project, all the congregations found this distinction hard to make. An exercise at the evaluation conference in April 1999 began to clarify their thinking. We explored news items from church magazines,

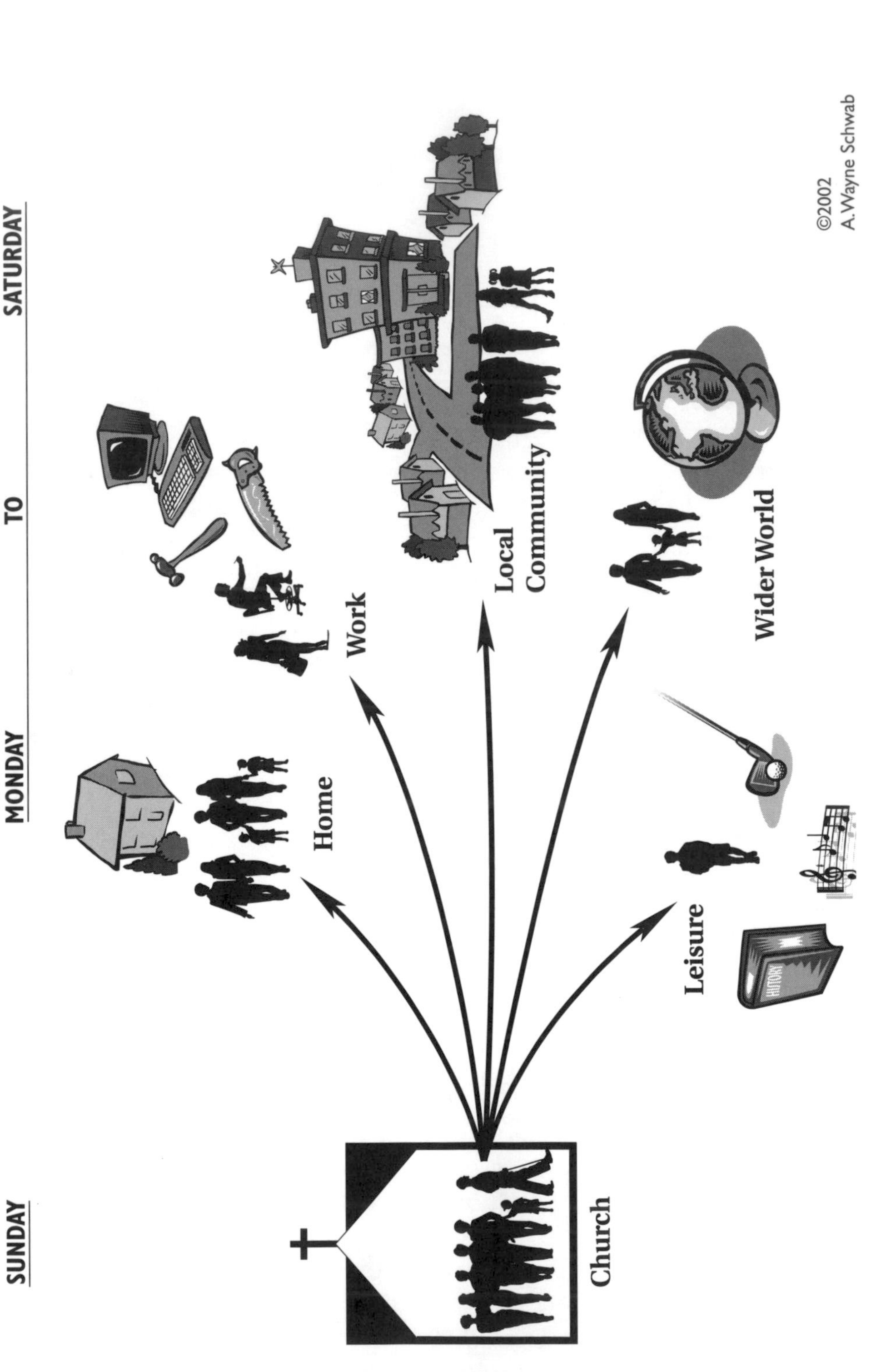

SUNDAY   MONDAY   TO   SATURDAY

Church

Home

Work

Local Community

Leisure

Wider World

What "Hubble-vision" Sees

©2002
A. Wayne Schwab

notices of special church programs, excerpts from noted church consultants, and newspaper ads. Each of these seemed to assume that the congregation was the only agent of mission. Each assumed "body-mission."
We asked what would have assumed "member-mission" and how might
that have found expression.

"Member-missions" are the missions members undertake in their daily
mission fields. The young mother who believes she should involve her
husband more deeply in infant care is on a member-mission. The repair
garage operator who believes he should seek health coverage for his workers is on a member-mission.

Here are illustrations from a consultation. The work was done with a
group seeking to learn to use "Hubble-vision." An Easter ad in the congregation's local newspaper gave the usual list of special services and
music. We noted its wholly church-centered language. Then, we asked
what one line could have been added to suggest that this congregation's
Easter schedule sought to help each member live each moment as a missionary of Jesus Christ.

Another congregation announced "Building Stronger Christians," a two-
day conference. But what were the Christians being strengthened for —
building up the church or building up the world? Suppose plans were
revised to center on member-mission. We tried rewriting the title to show
how Christians were to be strengthened for their daily mission fields.
Quickly, someone said, "Building Stronger Christians for
Daily Living." Just as quickly, another shortened it to "Building
Stronger Missionaries."

The Living Church (January 24, 1999) reported an Episcopal diocesan
conference on "A Clear Vision of One Church" with "presentations on congregational development, college ministry, prison ministry, and various
outreach programs." We tried to name two presentations that would have
been devoted, explicitly, to what the members do in their daily arenas.
"New Ways in Parenting" and "Traits of Christian Managers" were named.

In *The Once and Future Church* (The Alban Institute, 1991), Loren B.
Mead calls the laity "our primary mission officers" (p. 56) as congregations move from maintenance to mission. Yet, in the next chapter, he
points to "congregational studies" (p. 69) as the place to look for how to
move into the future. Such examinations center on what the congregation
does, not the daily missions of the members.

Carl Dudley in *Making the Small Church Effective* (1978, p. 124) writes: "Small congregations distinguished themselves in their emphasis upon a Christ-centered faith, the importance of Christian fellowship, and the urgency to respond to people in need." We asked what might small churches do to "distinguish" themselves as helping their members to live as Christians in each of their daily arenas.

As congregational leaders begin to distinguish between member-mission and body-mission, ask them which is most likely to effect substantive change. The laity in their homes, in their workplaces from the drive-by window to the assembly line to the boardroom, and in their elected, appointed, or volunteer government and community roles have access to the power to make those places more just and more caring. The relief of human need by congregations and the programs and resolutions of deaneries, dioceses, and national bodies often play only a limited part in achieving some needed change. Task groups, programs, and resolutions are limited by not being part of the home, the corporation, or the arm of government where the changes can actually be made. At times, as in the civil rights struggle of the fifties and sixties, resolutions and demonstrations can make a difference. Still, honesty suggests that body-missions function more as signs of God's call for change. Usually, they are not the effective agents of that call for change. Being a sign of God's will has power. Congregations become such a powerful sign when they center on struggles for caring and justice at work, in the home, or in community and civic life.

Church leaders like to talk about the congregation as a Christian outpost in the struggle against evil. The true outpost is each daily arena of the lay person. The congregation is the place of rest and rehabilitation offering sacramental ways to reconnect with God's restoration and power. The congregation is the place to once again find direction and power and to acquire more skill for Monday to Saturday mission.

If leaders are not vigilant about the primacy of member-mission, they will be drawn again and again into body-mission without knowing it. To be able to distinguish member-mission from body-mission is to be able to resist the congregation's constant tendency to ignore the missions of its members.

Redesigning the congregation is everyone's job

Redesign is a game all get to play! Not everyone will be ready to join the leaders when they begin to question just what kind of members their congregation is producing. Meet resistance with reason and resolve: "Surely we know that, above all, Jesus was most concerned about how we live. The Kingdom of God was about God's reign in all of life. We must put first helping our members to live and work for the reign of God in all of life! We will not lose anything of value. We do want to refocus everything we do around how our members live from day to day." Do not override resistance; learn from it. What counts for leaders is to start the redesign knowing and saying repeatedly that the redesign is everyone's job.

The leader forms a team

The leader begins by forming a team. Two can be enough but three to four is better in a small congregation. In larger congregations, up to five or six is enough. Present the vision. Perhaps, use parts of this book that will appeal to the prospective teammates. Describe the task of the team as sharing in decision making and in communicating decisions to the congregation. Anticipate team building as the team's first task. When all have been recruited, decide together how and where to meet.

Begin team building by agreeing to six sessions to share the present missions of each person in each daily arena. Prepare for each session by working through the seven questions for that mission field (see Appendix A) selected for that session. Begin each session with the oral Bible study method (see pp. 165-167). Then, each person shares his or her description of the selected mission field. Plan for sessions of about ninety minutes for a team of five. This approach serves several purposes. Members meet each other at a deeper, more intimate level. They meet doing what they want every member of the congregation to do. They build a common language and clarify basic procedures. For example, they will begin to see just how specific their present missions are and the need to be that specific. Most of all, they grasp afresh a sense of God's presence in every moment of daily life.

Expand the team by involving the church leadership. One place to start may be with the orientation of new members. Just what does the church council or vestry want offered to new members? Find some way to involve them in exploring and deciding what should be offered. For example, put fifteen minutes of exploration on the agenda of each meeting. Meeting by meeting, take up questions like these one by one.

What is participation in the congregation giving members now?

What do we suppose God wants participation to give members?

What is the place of our daily living in our sense of what God wants?

What will help us to offer what we sense God wants members to receive?

Two issues underlie whatever questions are asked. The first is just what are we producing? Are we producing compliant, loyal members or missionaries? The second is just what do we want to produce? Do we want to produce more compliant, loyal members or more missionaries? Finally, at each meeting, include some form of biblical reflection that links the passage to daily life. Whatever approach is used to redesign the congregation, the leader must find appropriate ways and words to keep the leaders and the congregation informed about what is being done. ✦

Chapter 10 — Let's Redesign

Begin by finding the congregation's *lived* purpose

Determine the congregation's actual purpose. Do not assume the congregation's mission statement answers the question. Find the *lived* purpose, not the *stated* purpose. Gather a representative group of leaders and members. State the purpose of the meeting clearly when you invite them and when you start the meeting. "Let's talk about what we are doing as a congregation and why. The clearer all of us are on what we are doing and why, the more effective we will be."

Have large note pads at hand on an easel. Follow these steps.

1. List everything happening in the life of the congregation. Be thorough. Even a small congregation can fill the whole sheet.

2. Ask to what extent all of these things are intertwined and working together. Be honest.

3. Ask what seems to be the working purpose of the congregation that binds all of these activities together. Allow a few minutes for silent reflection. Next, ask each to pair up with the person next to her or him and share with each other their answers. Now, go back to a meeting of the whole and ask for their answers. Write down every answer offered. Test for a common or underlying theme.

4. Reflect together on the group's work, asking for what has been learned.

5. Repeat the purpose of the session and announce the next step: "We need to put all this together into a vision of where we are going. This is the first step. We will propose a vision that, we pray, will both attract and motivate. Actually, our visioning will be ongoing. We will come up with a proposal, modify it with your help, and start to use it. We will review it from time to time to improve it as we live and work with it. Those working with me are (name the members of your leadership team). Share your comments with any of us at any time. Thanks so much for coming."

The leader develops an initial vision

The leader of the congregation has the central role in the visioning. But, control is not the issue; vitality is. State the vision succinctly — ideally, in one sentence. It should point to the goal — every member as a missionary. If possible, build on the language of the working purpose that came out of the meeting described above.

Share the vision with the leadership team. Revise and test it many times with them. Then, try it with the church council. Share the vision at every meeting of any kind. Each time, note any feedback and keep revising the vision so that it works for everyone. Remember that every meeting should begin with a recall of the current version of the vision by the leader of the meeting. Every place the congregation's name appears, try to follow it with the vision or some part of it — on stationery, publications, signs, news releases, and publicity of any kind.

For example, the current letterhead of St. John's, Essex, New York, reads, "A congregation of the Episcopal Diocese of Albany sharing in God's work of calling, forming, sending, and supporting Christians as agents of love and justice as known in Jesus Christ." A recent formal vision statement of St. John's reads: "At St. John's Episcopal Church in Essex, New York, we all share in God's work of calling, forming, sending, and supporting Christians as agents of love and justice as known in Jesus Christ. We seek to live this way in every part of daily life: home, work, local community, wider world, leisure, and church." The rector began the visioning process about three years ago. This wording of the vision began to emerge after about two and a half years of testing and feedback.

A theory of congregational life

At this point, the redesign needs a theory of congregational life adapted to this era. When the members are the primary missionaries, congregational life must have four basic dimensions to sustain this vision in today's world.

> **Mission** — the individual members bring good news in deed and word to life's daily arenas; and the members join together in missions to build up their community and wider world in the name of the congregation.

> **Formation for mission** — the congregation helps prospective members to become part of the mission.

Worship — the heartland of all Christian life as through weekly word and sacrament, the members clarify their vision of their missions, receive power to live them, and heed the call to return to their mission fields in the world.

Support for Mission — the members come together to support one another in their individual and corporate missions.

Each basic dimension finds expression in a basic activity.

Mission is expressed in *calling* individual people and situations and structures to more loving and just patterns and in calling individuals to join the mission of Jesus Christ.

Formation for mission is expressed in *forming* individuals as missionaries of Jesus Christ through regular worship, regular reflection on scripture and daily life, discovery of their daily missions, and participation in service and justice ministries.

Worship gives expression to *sending* each of the baptized on mission for Jesus Christ; in baptism and its related rites one joins and continues in the mission; and each eucharist reenacts baptism as worshipers, with their Lord, are broken for the world.

Supporting mission finds strong expression as the members meet in ongoing small groups to reflect on scripture and daily life, to pray for one another, and to develop their skills.

Figure 2 illustrates these dimensions and the activities giving them expression.

These dimensions and their activities can be carried on effectively by any size congregation. All the other things congregations do — bazaars, dinners, fellowship groups, etc. — are secondary. Let us examine each activity in closer detail.

Calling

Calling to join the mission of Jesus Christ is done by members in their daily mission fields. Calling happens in a variety of ways — most of them implicit rather than explicit. Discern them by discerning all love and justice as the work of God among us. Christians are quite familiar with much of God's work being hidden and unrecognized. So, when Christians are loving and just in any of their daily arenas, their behavior is an implicit call to those around them to respond in like manner and so share in God's work without their knowing it. When Christians work to change unlov-

MISSION

Baptized members, in each of their daily arenas,
are loving and just and offer commitment
to Jesus Christ. Congregation builds up its
community and the wider world, protects the
environment, and offers the Christian way.

Calling

WORSHIP

Heartland of Christian living for
direction and power

Sending

SUPPORT FOR MISSION

Small groups for biblical
reflection and regional
workshops for affinity groups

Supporting

FORMATION FOR MISSION

Learning Christian living in
worship, in one's daily mission fields,
and in Christian community

Forming

**The Four Dimensions of Congregational Life
That Sustain Members as Missionaries
Figure 2**

©2002
A. Wayne Schwab

ing or unjust situations or structures and the participants in these situations or structures, they are calling the people, the structures, and the forces at work in these situations to move toward the love and justice of God's mission. We properly see the improvement of faulty voting procedures on election day as a work of the Lord of justice as much as it is a work of the people working for the change. Further, when Christians ask others to join them in working for caring and fairness anywhere, they are calling them to be implicit agents of God's mission.

The implicit needs to become explicit. Therefore, Christians are ever watchful for chances to point to God's place in the changes sought and in the power needed to achieve them. The more explicit they become, the more clearly they call others to be conscious agents of God's reign in Jesus Christ. Question #6 (see p. 11) in discerning your daily missions is designed to prepare the missionary to meet this opportunity. The calling is not complete until the Christian has said something like, "I find in Jesus Christ the leads and the power I need to do this work. You might find the same. Would you come with me to church Sunday to pray for what we are doing?" Question #7 (p. 11) is designed to help the missionary be ready to talk this way. Christian mission is incomplete until such an explicit call or invitation is made. While chances to talk this way are few, the Christian is ever watchful for them.

Calling also occurs as the members work together in body-missions to build up their community and the wider world. They both respond to the physical, emotional, and spiritual needs of individual people and, remembering justice is the public face of love, they work for a more just society and environmental sustainabilty. As they work with or meet nonchurch people, the members look for ways to point to and to commend Jesus Christ as guide and helper for all. Again, remember, young adults are more likely to connect — or reconnect — with God-talk and church life, first, through a congregation's works of justice or caring. Worship and biblical reflection on daily life are more likely to follow such contact than precede it.

In both member-missions and body-missions, the "call" always suggests some part of the life of Jesus' people that might appeal to that particular person. The member also offers to accompany the seeker. Members make sure that loving and just deeds come first and provide the framework for their talk of God and joining God's mission. Therefore, redesign of church life needs to plan ways to train members in offering a call or invitation.

More conventional means of calling people to join the mission are door-to-door visiting, hospitality and follow-up for Sunday visitors, courses, weekend conferences, publicity, telephone canvassing, adequate church signs, and preaching missions. In each, the members need to be able to describe the congregation's mission, what its worship offers, and the Gospel itself in one or two sentences. When asked, they should be ready to share their own experiences in mission, worship, and living the Gospel. Keep in mind that all publicity and advertising should reflect the congregation's focus on the members as the primary missionaries.

Forming

Becoming a missionary takes more than listening for new knowledge. One takes on a deeper, if not new, lifestyle. Day by day and week by week, the missionary-to-be needs the companionship of members who are already living their missions. Together, they worship, reflect on scripture and daily life, discern their daily missions, and share in service and justice ministries. In recent years, we use the words "forming" and "formation" to refer to this community-centered learning. Formation is participating in and practicing the life of faith. Together, seeker and members move through this formation. Rites mark the stages of the candidate's development as a missionary. baptism into the mission of Jesus Christ completes the initial formation. Reaffirmation (also known as "confirmation") of their baptismal promises helps to maintain the initial formation of those already baptized. See Chapter 13, "Helping People to Become Missionaries," for a full development of formation.

Sending

Sending the newly formed or refreshed missionaries into the mission of Jesus Christ occurs in Holy Baptism or reaffirmation of Baptismal Vows. To speak of baptism as joining the mission of Jesus Christ goes beyond many of the existing definitions of baptism. For example, the Episcopal Outline of the Faith talks of baptism as "the sacrament by which God adopts us as his children and makes us members of Christ's Body, the Church, and inheritors of the kingdom of God" (BCP, p. 858). That traditional language does not go back far enough. It seems to place primary emphasis on membership. In the past fifty years, the church has recovered the historic sense of baptism as entry into a whole new way of living. The renunciations, promises, and covenant of the 1979 Episcopal rite place the baptized in the framework of mission, rather than membership. Baptism is dying to an old life and being raised to a new life in Jesus Christ. This meaning of baptism demands talk of mission, not just membership. Commitment to church membership is part of the commitment to mission — God's mission. Sending continues in each Sunday's eucharist. In the early centuries, baptism ended at Jesus' table receiving the bread and wine of the eucharist with one's new sisters and brothers in Christ. Therefore, every eucharist repeats one's baptism.

Obviously, to speak of baptism as joining the mission of Jesus Christ challenges our accustomed practices of infant baptism. Adult baptism should be the model guiding our preparation of parents and godparents for the baptism of infants and young children. Infant baptism is, ideally, a pastoral exception for the children of believing parents. This insight jars most of us who are new to this in-depth view of baptism. Leaders cannot blame members for the inadequate teaching they have been given in the past. Accept people where they are. Just begin the preparation with talk of baptism as joining the mission and build on that foundation. My own experience shows this not only works but is well received by the parents and godparents (see Appendix C).

Supporting

Small groups are, probably, the best support for both new and ongoing missionaries. In a small group, all the members can reflect on their specific and current missions in the light of a Bible passage. These gatherings end with prayers for each person based on the missions each senses God is calling him or her to take up. The next session begins with each sharing what happened in the mission he or she talked about at the last session. Some come ready to share specific answers to the prayers offered. Others begin to see answers to prayers they had overlooked until now. The sense of God's constant presence and help for each person grows as the meetings progress. (See Chapter 15, "Some Specifics About Small Groups," for more.)

Periodic regional gatherings can offer special insight and support for specific missions. These meetings can range from workshops for elected officials, to workshops for managers, to sessions for wardens of congregations.

Sunday's celebration of word and sacrament abides as the primary source of direction and power for living. Incidentally, worship planners do well to ask constantly how each part of the eucharist reflects a primary focus on the daily missions of the members. (See Chapter 16, "How Worship and Preaching Can Nurture the Vision," for more.)

Changes this vision calls for throughout a communion

This vision for mission causes wonder as to what changes are called for beyond the congregation. How might the diocese or synod or district reflect this vision in its organization and purpose? How might the nation-wide communion reflect this vision in its organization and purpose? Congregational leaders can be helped to connect with regional and national church bodies by seeing how those bodies might function if they were organized around this vision. This does not mean congregational leaders must set to work changing the church around them. The harsh reality is that diocesan and national bodies are far from believing they exist, first, to support the missions of the members in their daily arenas. Congregational leaders need a clear picture of their own work and what the work of their regional and national bodies would be if they held this vision of the laity as the primary missionaries. Then, leaders can sift through the requests from these regional and national bodies with greater freedom and less guilt when they say no to various requests.

The following diagrams are offered to give congregational leaders a way to cope with the structural complexities and multiple demands that come from the wider church. The diagrams are adapted from a presentation by Ezra Earl Jones for a national Episcopal evangelism team meeting. An adaptation of the vision to the work of the congregation in its own community and in the wider world might be illustrated as in Figure 3.

©2002
A. Wayne Schwab

An Adapted Vision of the Congregation
Figure 3

The congregation looks to the regional body — diocese or synod or the like — to provide and to support competent leaders for their congregations. A symbol for the chief role of the regional body is the ordaining of clergy. In the Episcopal Church, the diocese selects and guides the training of candidates for ordination. Once ordained, the clergy look to the diocese for help to implement the vision in the congregations they serve. This vision at the level of the regional structure might be illustrated as in Figure 4.

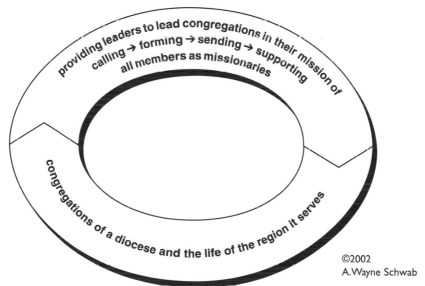

©2002
A. Wayne Schwab

The Vision Adapted to the Level of the Regional Church Structure
Figure 4

Regional bodies look to their national communion or fellowship for guidance and support in providing and supporting such leaders. The national communion and the structures it creates respond in a variety of ways. Guided by its tradition, the national body interprets who the communion is in belief and worship, how its members live, and how its members can cope with issues before it at the time. These responses and interpretations set boundaries and offer support within which dioceses or regional bodies lead their congregations in realizing the vision of the communion or fellowship might be illustrated as in Figure 5.

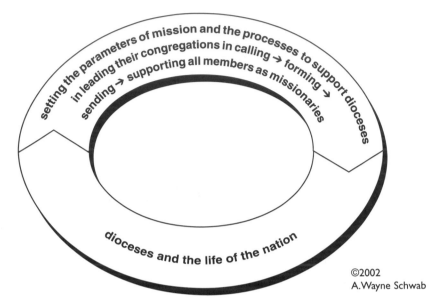

setting the parameters of mission and the processes to support dioceses in leading their congregations in calling → forming → sending → supporting all members as missionaries

dioceses and the life of the nation

©2002
A. Wayne Schwab

The Vision Adapted to the Level of a National Communion
Figure 5

These diagrams are only theoretical. Again, they are offered to help congregational teams assess how to work with the church systems beyond them without being victimized by them.

Concrete next steps for congregations follow in the chapters on formation for mission, working for change, small groups, worship and leadership. Before turning to them, we must deal with Christian decision making and spirituality. ✦

Chapter 11 — Decision Making for the Missionaries

Once a mission is chosen, countless decisions have to be made to achieve it. Indeed, the mission itself is chosen from among several alternatives. When Christians work through each of their current missions, they need clear and direct guidelines. Something like the following guidelines should be part of newcomers' orientation and preparation for baptism and for confirmation or reaffirmation.

Some givens

1. Keep in mind that every situation is unique. The experience of others can inform the decision maker and describe what has been done in similar settings. However, the experience of others does not determine the decision to be made.

2. The decision maker should make her or his own decisions and be responsible for the consequences. Others may share in that responsibility, but this responsibility does not remove the degree of responsibility appropriate to the decision maker.

3. Often, a choice between different degrees of good and evil is necessary. Sometimes those degrees do not differ very much. Further, the alternatives often contain worthwhile values that compete with each other.

Basic Christian values

1. Love in face-to-face relationships.
2. Justice in social relationships.

Five factors in Christian decision making

1. Alternatives. Outline all the possible choices. Then, examine each alternative for the motives at work, the ends sought, the means used to achieve them, and the likely outcomes.

2. Motives. To what extent do our motives participate in love or justice? Work to be honest about self-serving, hidden, or unconscious motives.

3   Ends. To what extent are the goals loving or just?

4. Means. How loving or just are the means used to achieve the end(s)?

5. Outcomes. To what extent will each outcome be a more loving or just situation for all who are involved?

Sources of counsel for Christians

1. From scripture: Are the five factors in accord with scriptural teaching and insight?

2. From non-Christian experts in the field: Others do not have to know God for God to use them; knowing that they have no monopoly on wisdom, Christians seek the best guidance available.

3. From Christian friends: How do one's Christian friends see it?

4. From inner guidance: Sometimes a clear sense of God's will emerges; sometimes the best decision is an intuitive one where one follows an inner sense that "this is the way to go."

5. Through prayer: Choose and offer your decision to God asking God to adopt what is right and to correct and overcome what is wrong.

Two examples

Most decisions are made without full knowledge of all the alternatives, motives, ends, means, and outcomes known to the decision maker. Accordingly, the risk of error is practically unavoidable. Nevertheless, weighing these five factors can be useful. Kit and Eddie, whose stories appear in Part One, weighed the options and chose the course of action described. A chart of how they might have weighed the five factors in reaching their decision follows. While it is hypothetical, it illustrates several realities in decision making: there are usually more than two alternatives; looking at each factor can bring out issues that might otherwise be overlooked; and one can see new elements in the same situation each time one reviews all the factors involved.

Key: follow one letter at a time through the five steps in each situation.

Kit	Eddie
Situation: a working mother feels too pressured	*Situation:* when cases go badly, lawyers meet only blame

1. Alternatives – list all realistic ones

a. Quit her job	a. Support lawyers who did not do well as best I can
b. Seek extended counseling about what to do	b. Work with supervisors to go easier on mistake makers
c. Find some way to take quiet time	c. Explore what went wrong; no blame

2. Motives – be honest; test how loving/just each is

a. Satisfaction of fighting back	a. They get some sympathy
b. Get someone on my side	b. Prevent discouragement
c. Sooner or later, I need to cope on my own	c. Make it a learning experience

3. Ends – test how loving/just is each end sought

a. No job demands	a. Temporarily eases pain
b. A helper I can count on	b. Less demanding supervisors
c. Tap unused resources of my own	c. Better work done by all

4. Means – test how loving/just is each method

a. Does not take account of the extent the rest of the family needs my income	a. Avoids mistake maker taking appropriate responsibility
b. A good counselor will help me grow	b. Supervisors do not get to what really went wrong
c. Good to develop my own resources	c. Affirms mistake maker

5. Outcomes – test how loving/just are results to all who are involved

a. May cost us all in ways I do not foresee	a. Mistake maker does not know how not to repeat mistake
b. My growth will make things better for the rest of the family	b. Supervisors don't see the real problem
c. I'm more balanced and I did it – with God's help	c. Mistake maker grows in skills

Among writers in Christian ethics, Alasdair MacIntyre (*After Virtue*, Notre Dame, 1984) and Stanley Hauerwas (*The Peaceable Kingdom*, Notre Dame, 1983) center on Christian community and building Christian character. In *Religion and Values in Public Life*, Summer 1997 (Harvard Divinity School), Lisa Sowle Cahill and Robin W. Lovin have called for a return to guiding the faithful in the specifics of daily Christian decision making. Earlier works in this direction are Earl H. Brill's *The Christian Moral Vision* (Harper & Row, 1979) and *The Anglican Moral Choice*, Paul Elman, ed. (Morehouse Publishing, 1983). ✦

Chapter 12 — Missionary Spirituality: The Kind That Supports Missionaries

The action research project underlying this book (see Preface) needed a title. In my reading, I came upon "missionary spirituality." An Australian church leader had used it to point to the mind-set he believed would help the church move from maintenance to mission. It seemed an apt name for the project. Spirituality is a popular quest, but the quest has not borne fruit in effective change.

The spiritually aware are not known for making private and public life more caring and fair. The kind of spirituality practiced does not seem to change the quality of private and public life. It lacks a "missionary" quality. It lacks the transformation of private and public life to be in accordance with the reign of God in Jesus Christ. We need a "missionary spirituality."

Individualism blocks the way

One serious obstacle is the prevailing cult of individualism in our society. Many people come to Sunday liturgies to satisfy their own preconceived religious needs. They seek a kind of "religious therapy." Spirituality is understood in terms of "God and me, period." Participation in a congregation is based on how it makes one "feel." When what happens on Sunday morning is not what one wants or expects, one "shops" elsewhere for the "package" one wants, more as a consumer than as a reliable agent of Jesus' mission.

The church has not really taught that each of us is on mission to transform those parts of the world in which we move. We have not really taught that we gather for mutual support and to refresh our sense of direction and to find the power to pursue it. At best, many congregations are self-supporting religious fellowships of individuals who band together to relieve suffering where they can. We do not find committed Christians making significant impact on society and culture in, for example, family-based education for mature sexuality; adequate health care for all; and an economy that seeks to put the worker ahead of profit. We are not coping with the culture's individualistic spin on spirituality.

A misleading spirituality

Part of the problem is not the culture's, but our own. What kind of spirituality do we really teach? Owen C. Thomas, Professor of Theology Emeritus at the Episcopal Divinity School, Cambridge, Massachusetts; and adjunct professor at the Graduate Theological Union, Berkeley, California, has pinpointed some of the serious problems in today's Christian spirituality in *The Anglican Theological Review*, (Volume LXXXII:2, Spring 2000). He writes:

> It is commonly assumed that spirituality is an optional matter, that some people are more spiritual than others and some not at all, that spirituality is essentially a good thing (the more spirituality the better), that while spirituality is somehow related to religion it should be sharply distinguished from religion as something superior to and more important than religion, that spirituality is essentially a matter of the inner or interior life (while religion is a matter of the outer life), and that, therefore, spirituality is essentially concerned with private life, rather than public life . . . . These common assumptions are erroneous and lead to damaging results in contemporary spirituality . . . I believe that spirituality is something universally human, that all people are spiritual, that spirituality and religion are practically synonymous, that spirituality, therefore, is as much concerned with the outer life (of the body, community, institutions, liturgy, tradition, doctrine, ethics, and society) as with the inner, and that spirituality is as much concerned with the public life of citizenship and work as with private life.

For members to be missionaries, we need the kind of spirituality in which Thomas believes. The missionaries we want are as concerned about the outer life as they are about the inner life. On the one hand, they know that Christian living in the outer world is not possible apart from a vital life with God in the inner world. On the other hand, they are convinced that rich inner life with God is empty, if it is not matched by intense involvement in the outer world.

Exchange submission for a spirituality of partnership

What in our Christian practice inhibits our attempts to change the world around us? The Rev. Martin Smith, Superior of the Society of St. John the Evangelist in Cambridge, Massachusetts, aptly ascribes our inhibitions to a spirituality of submission. He contrasts submission with the ways that we, as "fellow creators who are also creatures," are partners and collaborators with God. He develops this contrast in his opening of the first of five meditations given at a retreat in September 1993. The following excerpts from a transcript of his opening remarks may encourage many to make the difficult move from a spirituality of submission to one of collaboration:

> William Temple said, "We are the early Christians." One thing we are still so poor at grasping is the reciprocity of our relationship with God; the nature of the mutuality that we have with God . . . .
>
> In scripture, there are lots of clues that haven't yet been followed up. For example, those texts which describe human beings as collaborators with God, as fellow workers, fellow laborers are seldom preached from or referred to. In fact, most people are hardly aware that there are many places where scripture speaks of ourselves and God as fellow workers, working together. "As we work together with God, we also urge you not to accept the grace of God in vain" (2 Cor 6:1). "For we are God's servants, working together" (1 Cor 3:9) and the Greek means working together with God — *sunergoi*, collaborators, fellow laborers . . . .
>
> In actual fact, most of us are more familiar with traditions that avoid the mystery of divine and human co-creative partnership by stressing one pole and minimizing the other . . . . I suppose Calvinism is the greatest exemplar of this tradition — a tradition which tends to have associated with it a spirituality of submission to a preordained divine will . . . . Thus, in these early experimental days of Christianity, we've tried to make it easy for ourselves by cutting the dilemma of divine partnership and saying, "Let's not call it partnership. Let's call it obedience. Let's call it submission. Let's call it dependence" . . . .
>
> Of course, there is another polar opposite view which is, maybe, a form of humanism which says, "No, God has released human beings to live autonomously in the world. It's entirely up to human beings to work things out both on the individual and on the collective levels. No, God is content to be an onlooker as we struggle and strive and create . . . ."

These theological positions have sinister counterparts in everyday spirituality. An everyday counterpart is the belief that God either controls or abandons you . . . .

But I suggest that scripture and the Christian tradition itself, the Christian mystery, is saying something quite different but much more difficult to grasp intellectually than either of these two positions which is that the mystery of our relationship with God is a co-creative partnership . . . . What we [must] do . . . is see if we can really imagine our relationship with God to leave behind some of these images of control and submission, control or abandonment, and think of a creative God who delights in our own co-creativity, a spontaneous God who delights in our own spontaneity, a free God who intends us to be free and yet also be in intimacy with God.

(Copyright 1994 by Cowley Publications. All rights reserved. Reproduced as *Co-Creators With God* and available from Cowley Publications, 28 Temple Place, Boston, MA 02111; www.cowley.org; 1-800-225-1534.)

A spirituality of submission can kill a missionary spirituality. Mission is action. Sometimes the action is assertive. Sometimes restraint is the appropriate action. Submission cuts the nerve of both kinds of action. The collaborative co-worker with God is the missionary we seek. This missionary collaborates with both God and God's creations — both people and nature. This collaboration has some interesting socioeconomic cutting edges. For white, middle-class men, collaboration with God can mean walking away from their socially conditioned mind-set of being in control and in power to ask what is God doing here that we need to join. On the other hand, the marginalized can, happily, embrace freedom and power as they collaborate with God, who calls them to use their God-given capacities to the fullest.

Review the seven questions for discerning our specific missions (pp. 10-11). The first calls for a lively relationship with God to discern God's works or words in each mission field. The next three — what blocks reconciliation, justice, and love, what change is needed, and what can the missionary take on — are the questions of co-workers preparing to join God's work in each field. The last three — how will the missionary form a team to effect the change, how to connect the change with God, and how to offer life with God's people as the best way to achieve the change — are the questions of co-workers whose inner and outer lives are one. A spiritual director might well ask seekers to complete these questions for each of their daily arenas. A review of the results would forge a profound link between spirituality and daily decision making.

Return to *Christus victor*

Spirituality and theology go hand in hand. Have the missionaries take a careful look at their understanding of what God has done in Jesus Christ to help them. The commonly voiced and commonly held notion is "Jesus Christ died for our sins." Just what does this mean? Various programs of evangelism teach the reply: "God made us. Sin separated us. Someone had to pay the price for sin. Jesus paid that price when he laid down his life for us on the cross. God has raised him to new life. Jesus is the bridge across which we can walk to new life with God."

In brief, Jesus paid the price for human sin. Accept his sacrifice for us and you enter the new life with God. A biblical text often quoted is "For the Son of Man came not to be served but to serve, and to give his life a ransom for many" (Mark 10:45). The theological name for this teaching is substitutionary atonement or the satisfaction theory of the atonement. Atonement is "at-one-ment." It is what God has done for us in Jesus Christ that restores us to being at-one with God. In this view of the atonement, Jesus "satisfies" God's justice. Someone had to pay or "satisfy" the price of death for human sin. Jesus "substitutes" for us when he dies.

Paul's phrase "Christ died for our sins" (1 Cor 15:3) is used frequently as a scriptural basis for substitutionary atonement. The late Raymond E. Brown, Auburn Distinguished Professor Emeritus of Biblical Studies at Union Theological Seminary in New York City, offered another interpretation of this passage. In a lecture series, "Our Knowledge About the Passion," at Virginia Theological Seminary, Alexandria, Virginia, in 1987 (Truro Tape Ministries, Fairfax, Virginia; available at the Bishop Payne Library, Virginia Theological Seminary), Brown moves away from the satisfaction theory or substitutionary atonement. Brown outlines Jesus' utter dependence on God in Mark's account of the Passion. This utter dependence on God made Jesus subject to the sins of those around him and so resulted in his death. Brown would seem to say, "Christ died, not in payment for our sins, but as a result of our sins."

> . . . For the first time, ever, in the ministry, he [Jesus] prays to God not as Father but simply as God, "My God, my God, why have you forsaken me?" Mark is clearly drawing on [the] psalms in developing a theology but still it is a theology of a kind of alienation. He is not being visibly helped by God and the psalm [is a psalm] of one who

has always been helped [but not now] . . . "I have always been helped before. Why not this time?" We may be touching there something close to his [Jesus'] gradual understanding of his death — namely, total dependence so that it seems now God is not going to help. And that notion of self-emptying which is so strong in Mark might be the very key that Paul will develop in "his dying — Paul's language — for the sins of the world." Perhaps, in the language of the Gospel, so that God might show his power and bring his kingdom about fully in one who had no other dependence left except his dependence on God.

In *Understanding the Faith of the Church* of the Episcopal *The Church's Teaching Series* (Seabury, 1979, pp. 150-151), Richard A. Norris, Emeritus Professor of Church History at Union Theological Seminary, criticizes notions of sacrifice and atonement "in which God punishes some people (or one person) so that others can get off the hook." He continues:

Moreover, it is for just this reason that sacrifice is closely tied up with expiation and making atonement. When persons are estranged from one another, when responsive trust gives place to hostility and fear, sin — which we have defined as denial or refusal of the "other" — is actively present. But how is sin dealt with? How is reconciliation, or atonement, effected? The answer is that sacrifice must be made. Each party to the relationship must bear the hurt of the other. Then, and only then, does forgiveness occur. Then, and only then, do the two stand together once again. They are enabled to share a common life again by first sharing a common death, by taking up the burden of each other's pain.

And this exactly is the meaning of what the Scriptures call expiatory or atoning sacrifice. Such a sacrifice is not an attempt by human beings to appease or placate an angry God. Nor is it an action in which God punishes some people (or one person) so that others can get off the hook. These interpretations of expiatory sacrifice — widespread though they have been — simply miss the point. Expiatory sacrifice is a single gesture or action in which two things happen together: God in his love takes upon himself the burden of human guilt and estrangement, while his people takes upon itself God's judgment of its sin. Mercy on the one hand, and the acceptance of judgment on the other; divine action and human action: these are the two constitutive factors in expiatory sacrifice, the sacrifice which covers sin. And it is just this sort of event which the early Christians saw in the death of Christ. (Reprinted by permission of the Domestic and

Foreign Missionary Society of the Protestant Episcopal Church in the USA.)

Actually, the satisfaction theory of atonement emerged as a later view of the atonement in Christian history. Gustav Aulen, a Bishop in the Church of Sweden and Professor of Systematic Theology at Lund University, Sweden, in *Christus Victor*, first published in 1930, recovered the earlier view of the atonement. It is the typical or "classic" view of the New Testament and its first interpreters. This earlier view of the atonement he calls *Christus victor*. In this earlier meaning of Jesus' life and death, Jesus is the valiant fighter against evil. His death on the cross makes clear the radical depth of evil. It kills the one fully loving and just person. His resurrection makes clear the unconquerable power of God overcoming even death. The baptized share in Jesus' victory and power through the gift of the Holy Spirit. To use the framework of this book, those who join Jesus' mission in baptism receive his power to struggle against evil. The Holy Spirit brings this power and unites the missionaries with Jesus, with the Father–Creator, and with the other missionaries.

Writing about "The Classic View of the Atonement" of Aulen in *Principles of Christian Theology* (Scribners, 1977, p. 318), John Macquarie, Lady Margaret Professor of Divinity at Oxford University, comments:

> The classic view of the atonement sees the work of Christ, finished on the cross, as a victory over all the powers that enslave man, and so a deliverance from evil. And perhaps it should be added that this victory is always to be understood as God's victory.

> The expression "the work of Christ finished on the cross" has been taken from Aulen, and it is worth quoting his own statement of why this expression is used. "It is intended to indicate the central place which the cross has in Christian faith, and also to emphasize that the cross must be seen in connection with the whole life of Christ. The cross summarizes the totality of his life and work." This statement of Aulen is entirely in agreement with our own remarks in the opening paragraphs of this chapter.

> The classic view of atonement is already clearly expressed in the New Testament. There we see the work of Jesus portrayed as a battle against the demons that afflict the life of man. His finished work on the cross is his complete triumph over these demonic, enslaving powers. St. Paul tells us that God "has delivered us from the kingdom of darkness and transferred us to the kingdom of his beloved Son" (Col 1:13). He has

abolished the claim of these dark powers over us: "this he set aside, nailing it to the cross" (Col 2:14). And he has thus utterly discomfited them, and taken away their power over man: "He disarmed the principalities and powers and made a public example of them, triumphing over them in him" (Col 2:15). The model of struggle, victory, and triumph comes through clearly, and this model is developed (sometimes by way of fantastic elaborations) in patristic theology. The main outline, however, remains constant. Man has fallen into the grip of dark powers; Christ comes into this situation, and battles against these powers; with his cross comes the overwhelming victory, bringing deliverance and new life to man.

James A. Carpenter, retired Professor of Systematic Theology from General Theological Seminary, says of Jesus' work, "Jesus stopped evil in himself." That phrase is a succinct summary of *Christus victor*. He draws on Leonard Hodgson's *Doctrine of the Atonement* (Scribners, 1951) for it.

When mission — bringing good news in deed and word to every corner of creation — is central, *Christus victor* is indispensable. Substitutionary atonement or the satisfaction theory just does not seem to know of an ongoing struggle with evil in Jesus' name. *Christus victor* does know the struggle against evil. When one asks what will I do to increase reconciliation, justice, and love in each of one's mission fields, one is joining Jesus' ongoing struggle.

The great good news is that the power to overcome evil is available. The struggle will continue until the end of the world when all life is caught up in God's life. Even more true is the presence of the power to cope with evil, to keep it at bay, and, in some places, to overcome it for a space of time — until the Last Day when evil is overcome for ever.

Christus victor opens the door for a missionary spirituality

How one understands Jesus' work for us is, therefore, central to a missionary spirituality. With substitutionary atonement, the struggle seems to be over already. Jesus has basically done it all for us. Champions of substitutionary atonement might rightly claim this is a caricature. However, the small attention its followers seem to pay to changing private and public life argues in favor of its accuracy. A *Christus victor* theology may well be the key that unlocks the door to release the members to be the missionaries.

Way beyond locked doors and keys to open them is the Holy Spirit. A missionary spirituality is ultimately the work of the Holy Spirit in each Christian and in each Christian community. The Holy Spirit continues Christ's struggle with evil in and through us. Recovering mission and each member as a missionary calls for fervent work on one hand and fervent prayer for an outpouring of the Holy Spirit on the other. ✦

Chapter 13 — Helping People to Become Missionaries

Helping people to become missionaries is, in a way, very simple: Call people to join the mission, nothing less. It is really that simple: "Follow me and I will make you fish for people" (Mark 1:17).

Luke 4:18 presents a Jesus who is on a mission, God's mission: "The Spirit of the Lord is upon me, because he has anointed me to bring good news to the poor. He has sent me to proclaim release to the captives and recovery of sight to the blind, to let the oppressed go free, to proclaim the year of the Lord's favor." To follow Jesus is to join him in mission, God's mission.

Helping people become missionaries is prescribed in Matthew 10:7-8a: "As you go, proclaim the good news, 'The kingdom of heaven has come near.' Cure the sick, cleanse the lepers, cast out demons." We are to challenge one another to take on missions of word and deed!

Becoming a missionary is costly: "Those who love their life lose it, and those who hate their life in this world will keep it for eternal life. Whoever serves me must follow me, and where I am, there will my servant be also" (John 12:25-26a).

How do we help people to become missionaries? We call them to join the costly mission of Jesus Christ. Yes, call them into the community of Jesus, the church. Yes, call them into personal relationship with Jesus Christ. Above all, call them into the mission. To put the call this way may seem new to many, but it is very old as the texts above bear witness.

Conversion is, then, leaving former ways of living to join the mission of Jesus Christ. It is a process of formation as a missionary. It is "completed" in baptism when seekers commit themselves to the mission of Jesus Christ and God seals and empowers them as "Christ's own forever" (p. 308, BCP). For adults already baptized, conversion to being on mission for Jesus Christ is "completed" in some kind of reaffirmation of their baptismal promises. In truth, conversion is never completed but continues throughout one's life — hence, the quotes around "completed." Conscious commitment to Christ's mission in baptism is the central moment in this ongoing journey in faith. Reaffirmation of the baptismal covenant relives that central moment of baptism. Preparation for baptism or reaffirmation must prepare people to commit themselves to be missionaries of Jesus Christ all the time wherever they are. While we do not usually talk of calling people to commitment and of conversion this way, it is time we recovered it.

What are people looking for? A purpose or meaning for life. People look for direction for daily living that grows out of that purpose. We have great capacities for love and for justice, but we need help to realize our capacities. Christians offer the word and sacrament of Jesus' table as the place to find that direction and power to follow that purpose.

Yes, be ready to offer the unconditional love of God made known in Jesus Christ. Yes, be ready to lead to sensing the infilling of the Holy Spirit. Yes, offer the generations of learning and prayer that Christians have amassed over the years. But central to our offering must be participation in the mission of Jesus Christ and the direction and power to live it daily.

Avoid some errors

Calling people to costly mission may sound radically different from current ways in evangelism. Actually, the call to costly mission includes all the current ways in evangelism while it avoids their errors. One error is a religious experience that does not lead to changed living. Calling people to costly mission calls them to a religious experience that changes the way they live. Another error is joyful discovery of God's love that does not bear fruit in work for justice. Calling people to costly mission calls them to a joyful discovery of God's love for all people that makes work for justice inescapable. We avoid the error of a childlike dependence to take up a mature collaboration with God to make all of the world a better place. To receive the kingdom of God as a child (see Mark 10:15) is to trust God to be like the good parent who is with us every moment as we work for a better world.

My own sense of encounter with God in Christ was in the discovery of being "at home" when I had never before felt "at home." That discovery came in the midst of encounter with the justice of God as proclaimed by the prophets and fulfilled in Jesus Christ. Everyone is entitled to this full encounter with both God's unceasing work for justice and God's unconditional love.

The words offered here are intended to guide individual Christians as they offer the Christian way to those they meet in their daily mission fields. These notes also guide the leaders and workers in the corporate or "body" missions of congregations and larger church bodies. In whatever form each presents the Christian way, the call to join the mission is the full call to present.

The "grown up" Christian

If a congregation truly wants people to become missionaries of Jesus Christ in daily life, they will be sure that the call to follow Jesus is the call to join his mission. We are called to grow up. We are called from being God's children to being mature co-workers and partners in God's work. Life as God's mature co-workers is the proper content of preparation for baptism. People baptized as infants or children reaffirm their vows to be mature missionaries in confirmation (see the Episcopal *Book of Common Prayer*, p. 412, or the Lutheran *Book of Worship*, Rubric #3, p. 198).

Face it. Jesus is really most interested in how we live every moment, Monday to Monday. He calls us to live lovingly and justly all the time. He gives us the power we need to live that way in the bread and the cup. Congregations must make sure that, wherever people meet them, people meet the call to join the mission. For example, announcements for Easter worship must go beyond "Celebrate the resurrection of Jesus Christ" to "Join Jesus' victory of love and justice." And, congregations and their members must be known for going beyond these words to deeds of love and justice in all of their daily places.

"Salvation" revisited

"Salvation" is one of the time-honored words for what Jesus Christ offers. It is often misunderstood as meaning that, where we deserved death for our sin, Jesus sacrificed himself in our behalf. This is substitutionary atonement again. Salvation is much better understood in the framework of *Christus victor* — Jesus, the victor, saves or frees us from the powers of evil, sin, and death.

Among the world's religions, Christianity is unique in its diagnosis of our problems. So often we know what we ought to do, but we lack the power to do it. Sooner or later, sin surfaces. In Greek, sin means "to miss the mark." Sooner or later, we fall short — "miss the mark" — of what God has asked us to do. Our capacities as human beings are astounding. Too often, however, we are unable to realize them in their fullness. We fall short in any of a thousand and one different ways. "Sin" describes this fact of life. We cannot make it on our own. We need help. Who or what saves us from "missing the mark"? Jesus brings us the help we need. He saves us by giving us the power to live as God asks us to live. The gift of the Holy Spirit at Pentecost clothes us with this "power from on high" (Luke 24:49). The power by which Jesus overcame sin is now given to us. Now, we can begin to "hit the mark" more than we "miss it." This vision of "salvation" is, indeed, good news!

All this may be good theology, but how do we say it all in words that people can easily understand and grasp? It is possible. Try talking this way: "Jesus is interested most of all in how we live. We should be loving and just all the time, wherever we are. But we need help to live that way. Jesus gives us the help we need! Jesus gives us the power we need." Of course, there is much more to be said. Those words are not the full story. They do point to the unique Christian offer of salvation. Jesus saves us by giving us the power we need to cope with falling short.

In *The World's Religions*, Harper, 1991, p. 335, Huston Smith, an expert in the religions of the world, distinguishes unique features of each faith. Of Christianity and Christians, he writes, "They had experienced Jesus' love and had become convinced that Jesus was God incarnate. Once that love reached them, it could not be stopped. Melting the barriers of the fear, guilt, and self, *it poured through them as if they were sluice gates [or spillways], augmenting the love they had hitherto felt for others* until the difference in degree became a difference in kind and a new quality, which the world has come to call Christian love, was born." [The italics emphasize Smith's words describing the receiving of power to do what we could not do on our own — the unique message Christians carry.]

Grow the mission, not the church

Evangelism today is often hard to distinguish from the membership drive of any organization. "Church growth" continues to attract a following. Even the 2000 General Convention of the Episcopal Church adopted "20/20: A Clear Vision" as its theme. The program commits Episcopalians to doubling their size by the year 2020. While the strategies include evangelism, recruiting innovative leaders, strengthening congregational life, emphasizing youth and campus ministries, and prayer, all seem directed toward the church, not the world.

The power of numbers to seduce is very strong. Is today's lure of numbers of members the age-old lure of power in modern dress? One way out is to learn to seek more missionaries, not more members. Grow the mission, not the church.

Declining membership statistics have concerned many denominations for years. Where numbers are not declining, the rate of growth is slowing. While participation in worship is growing — in the Episcopal Church, for example — churches no longer exercise the power and influence of the past. My colleague, Jim Anderson, says, "God is dismantling the church." It is a powerful phrase. It suggests that the loss of power and influence is not so much due to the world's perversity as to the perversity of the churches. Too many congregations and their parent bodies seem to be more centered on maintenance than mission. The members' daily missions receive almost no attention at all.

Lest we despair, turn to Jeremiah. Jeremiah saw Israel in decline and about to fall to Babylon. In his prophetic vision, he understood God to say, "And just as I have watched over them to pluck up and to break down, to overthrow, destroy, and bring evil, so I will watch over them to build and to plant" (Jer. 31:28).

This is good news for both the world and the church. What God dismantles, God re-mantles. There will be a "new heaven and a new earth" (Rev. 21:1). "See, I am making all things new" (Rev. 21:5).

Christian missionaries live in hope of tomorrow and bring that hope for a new tomorrow to each of their daily arenas. The basic promise is to all the world — "all things." The missionaries and the church as instruments of God's mission will be renewed as well.

Give a real "taste"

Responding to invitations to "come and taste," seekers deserve orientation to the purpose and stance of the congregation. Orientation sessions for newcomers must focus on the call to mission. Some newcomers will be unbaptized or have had no significant church experience. Others may have been active in other congregations but are new to seeing themselves as missionaries wherever they are. All of these newcomers will need some kind of orientation. One place to begin is with a summary of the Gospel that is clear about the mission: "Through Jesus Christ, God overcomes evil, sin, and death and works to bring the whole creation to fulfillment in the Holy Spirit. The mission is to love all and to seek justice for all and to talk with all of what God is doing in Jesus Christ. Join the mission through baptism and find the power to live it at Jesus' table."

During orientation, some of the members share their missions to transform their homes, their daily work, their local communities, the wider world, and their leisure, as well as their congregation. In this framework, the members also listen to the stories of the newcomers and what brought them to the congregation. Next, describe the heritage of the denomination and the congregation but as instruments of the mission, not its goal. The sessions conclude with encouraging newcomers to undertake their own formation as missionaries.

From seeker to missionary via the catechumenate

To be formed as a missionary, the seeker needs:

- ongoing experience and instruction in public and private worship;
- a Christian world view of the depth of our human need for help and God's response in Jesus Christ as expressed in *Christus victor*;
- small group experience of biblically based reflection on daily life;
- the basics of Christian decision making;
- the opportunity to discern their present missions in each of their daily arenas;
- participation in the service and justice ministries of the congregation and diocese or regional body;
- sponsors or companions who go through the process with them;
- liturgies or rites that express and further their growth in formation (see the next paragraphs); and,
- ever deepening relationships with members of the congregation and the Christian community as a whole.

One way to realize that full list is to follow "The Preparation of Adults for Holy baptism: The Catechumenate" in *The Book of Occasional Services: 1994* of the Episcopal Church (Church Publishing Inc., New York City, New York). The catechumenate arose during the early years of the Christian church as preparation for baptism. "Catechumen" comes from the Greek verb *katecheo* meaning "to cause to sound in the ear." This apt choice suggests Jesus the Word sounding in the inner ear of the candidate. Catechumens, candidates for baptism, spent up to three years in worship (up to the offertory) and weekly biblical reflection with their Christian sisters and brothers to be. Sharing in the congregation's service of others — the poor, orphans, prisoners — was equally mandatory during these three years. Their growth in insight and faith was marked by rites that both expressed their growth and supported their next steps.

In place by 150 A.D., some say early forms of the catechumenate underlie the shape of some of the Gospel material. In *Luke 1:1-9:50* (Concordia, 1996), Arthur A. Just, Jr., Professor of Exegetical Theology, Concordia Theological Seminary, Ft. Wayne, Indiana, interprets the first nine chapters of Luke's Gospel as shaped for use in the catechumenate. The catechumenate was recovered in the 1850s in French Equatorial Africa when church leaders sought a means to form new converts in the Christian faith. Nothing else seemed to give the converts sufficient grounding in Christian faith and living. It spread into Europe and the United States through Belgium in the 1940s and 1950s.

Vatican II initiated a process that resulted in the *Rite of Christian Initiation of Adults* published in 1972. It set forth procedures and rites for a catechumenate. The Episcopal Church established forms for a catechumenate in 1979, and Lutherans and Methodists began to develop their own adaptations of it in the early 1990s. The North American Association for the Catechumenate is a modest, but growing, organization of leaders and learners from the communions working with catechumenal formation. (See www.catechumenate.org for training events, resources, links to leaders and communions developing catechumenal formation, and information about an annual conference along with transcripts of addresses at past conferences.) Episcopal and Anglican Church of Canada, Lutheran (ELCA and the Canadian ELCIC), Methodist (UMC), Presbyterian (USA), Reformed Church, Roman Catholic, and United Church of Christ people participate to date. The catechumenate is national policy of the Anglican Church of Australia, where a national staff office supports the thirteen of its twenty-three dioceses already implementing it.

Today, a full three-year catechumenal process is hard to find. Most of the time, we have to focus on the absolute essentials in a much shorter time period. The months from September through May are often used. Those essentials should be:

- participation in public and private worship;
- a Christian world view of the depth of our human need for help and

God's response in Jesus Christ as expressed in *Christus victor*;

- the opportunity to discern their present missions in each of their daily arenas;

- small group experience of biblically based reflection on daily life; and

- the basic Christian ethic of love and justice, the public face of love.

These essentials can be worked on even in the shortest of formation periods. The optimum is some form of catechumenal formation with its distinct steps and rites and sponsors for each candidate.

Five steps in formation

There are five stages of catechumenal formation to keep in mind. Episcopalians have been describing them in such terms as these:

- *Inquiry*: to listen to the stories of the participants and the Christian story;

- *Formation*: to practice reflection on biblical passages and daily living — discerning their present missions occurs here;

- *Preparation*: to receive grace — the freely given love and help of God — and to commit oneself to Jesus Christ in baptism or reaffirmation of the baptismal covenant;

- *Commitment and empowerment*: in baptism or reaffirmation; and

- *Reflection*: reflecting on living as a newly baptized or reaffirmed person who regularly shares in the bread and the cup.

Ideally each stage is observed by a rite. The rites both express and increase growth in Christian commitment and living.

The Catechumenal Process: Adult Initiation & Formation for Christian Life and Ministry (Church Publishing, 1990) published by the Episcopal Church still works to guide leaders in formation. It is called "the yellow bible" in Australia and New Zealand. Too often, leaders use this resource — and others — in ways that leave participants inside the church. Excited by some form of religious experience and newfound knowledge, they still have little to no sense of how to be on mission once they leave the church. Therefore, it is important not to omit the following elements:

- Provide time for all people to discern and share their present missions in each of their daily arenas.

- For biblical reflection, try the Oral Method of Bible Study at least once. The Oral Method provides a setting for participants to discover God's work in their daily living. (See Chapter 15 for details.)

- During biblical reflection, listen for people to begin to talk of their mission fields. If one or more of the mission fields have not come up by the end of the second session, ask the participants to be prepared to seek what God is calling them to in one of their mission fields. In the next session, ask about home; in the next, ask about work; in the next, ask about leisure and church.

- Take care to look for and affirm behavioral change as the sessions progress (see pp. 64- 65, 69-70, and 73 of *The Catechumenal Process*).

- As you use the rites, provide some way for both the participants and the congregation to reflect together on their experience of the rites.

Companions in the way

Maintain these treasured people through vital mission support. That means small groups for ongoing biblical reflection and mutual sharing of daily missions (Chapter 15). That means corporate worship that both directs and empowers the missionaries (Chapter 16). Without support, their conscious attention to mission will probably wither away. Jesus sent out the twelve and the seventy two-by-two. We all need companions in the way.

Companions for the lapsed, too

The vision of the members as today's missionaries provides a new way to approach and reach lapsed members. Let go of the usual goal to get them "back into the church." A new and more vital goal is to support them in their present mission fields. Visit with them to learn the shape of their present mission fields. They may not see their six daily arenas as mission fields. Nevertheless, they cope with specific issues in each one. Ask them: "How are things going at home? at work? in the community?" As you listen for the answers, you will hear what they are coping with in each arena. You are hearing their present mission in each arena, even if they do not see it as mission. God is there even if they do not have eyes to see or ears to hear. Their baptism has not been revoked. They may have lapsed in church participation but their call to mission has not lapsed. Become one of their companions offering concern, insight, and prayer support.

Encourage them to discover or rediscover worship as a place for direction and power. Mentioning worship may well bring up past hurts, disappointments, or disagreements that led to their lapse. Be ready to take the time to work through painful experiences in later visits. For further insight, turn to the wealth of material on helping the lapsed to return. However, never lose sight of your basic goal to support their current missions. If they are in the pew next Sunday, great! Still, if they are not there on Sunday but start Monday with a new sense of purpose and of God at work through them, you have more than succeeded!

Visiting lapsed members in this manner can bear rich fruit. We promised to "do all in (our) power to support this person in her/his life in Christ" at their baptism. In the Holy Spirit, we are one with those original promise makers. Such visits keep that promise. The clergy cannot do this visiting alone. A growing group of visitors who meet regularly to share and reflect on their visits can begin to move toward the goal of such visits with each of the lapsed once a year.

What about the rest of the congregation?

As a congregation moves into its new stance of the members as missionaries, the present members will, probably, need to experience the same orientation. Then they will be more able to talk with seekers and newcomers about the congregation's new direction. Further, they might want to join with newcomers undertaking formation as missionaries. In all likelihood, most present members have never experienced such formation themselves.

Try to involve the rest of the congregation in, at least, two dimensions of this formation. Give them a taste of biblical reflection that connects with living our missions in our daily arenas. Also, give them practice in discerning one of their present concerns or goals as a mission. If possible, work through the seven questions for one of their mission fields.

For members of the redesign team, see the suggestions on page 117. For core leaders, include this kind of biblical reflection in several of their regular meetings. In a workshop, also introduce them to discerning their work on one or more of their present concerns and goals as missions. I have found this procedure also works well in baptismal preparation. (See Appendix C for such a format.) It both affirms the missionary notes of their concerns and gives them a chance to connect biblical concepts with their concerns. Further, as soon as possible, begin at least one group for regular biblical reflection on daily life. (See Chapter 15.) Offer repeated invitations to all members of the congregation to visit this group at least twice to get a feel for this viewpoint. Also invite newcomers and visitors to participate in this group, at least twice, as well. Finally, make available to all summaries of this vision of the members as the missionaries and how corporate worship expresses and supports it. (For samples, see Appendix D.) ✦

Chapter 14 — Change Agents at Work

Change begins at home

A clear, specific goal or vision is the best way to start to change things. Work through the seven questions to discern your mission in each of your mission fields with care. Question #4, about what you will do, is the place to be clear and specific. The questions up to #4 help you get to the specifics. The questions after #4 help you to carry out your vision. As you work, follow these hints for each question. Finally, remember that the duration of a mission may be brief or lengthy. When a mission is completed, look for your next mission in this field.

Question #1: What has God been telling me or doing through my life in this mission field?

Begin with looking or listening for what God is already doing or saying to you in this arena. Problems do not seem to be as big when we sense where God is already at work.

Questions #2 and #3: What conditions inhibit reconciliation, justice, and love (peacemaking, fairness, and caring) in this mission field? What change is needed to increase reconciliation, justice, and love (peacemaking, fairness, and caring) in this mission field?

Analyze the underlying problem. Dig below symptoms to the root causes. Keep asking is this the real cause or is there something deeper. Keep probing for what, if done, will really make a change.

Question #4: What will I do to achieve this change considering my gifts, limitations, and convictions?

Choose what you really can do. You are not super-person. Adapt what you will do around your talents, interests, gifts, and passions.

Question #5: What vision (description of what I will do) will I use to draw others into working with me for this change?

Word your vision to attract others to join you to work for the change. We can be so aware of a needed change, we forget others may not see it as clearly as we do. They not only need to see it. They need to be captivated by it. Martin Luther King wanted to enlist everyone in removing racial barriers. His "I Have a Dream" speech still echoes in the ears of those of us who experienced the sixties directly. Each of the storytellers in Part 1 had an attractive vision. Look for teammates. Your team will be a community. It is a kind of little church. Your teammates will be answering a "call" to share in your mission. The "lone ranger" syndrome dies hard. Each of us needs allies as we work for change. We need to find them and we need to cultivate them. Stay in touch. Test possible courses of action with one another. Reflect as a team on what has happened and what next steps might be taken.

Question #6: How will I talk of God while I am sharing my vision (what I plan to do) or following through on it?

Work through how you will link God to the change that is needed. Do not parade the connection, but do look for occasions to spell it out. The spiritually aware will be heartened that you see the depth of the situation. The nonreligious may be intrigued to hear God named outside a "churchy" context. As noted earlier, a professor at a teachers' college said, "I believe helping students is part of teaching." The teacher was known among students for being a regular communicant. Some heard "I believe" as a faith statement.

Question #7: How will I invite others to join me at Jesus' table to be fed and empowered to achieve this vision? (How will I encourage others to seek help in church life?)

Be ready to encourage others to find direction and power for the vision by seeking out the people who gather at Jesus' table. And, offer to accompany them when they come. People with no church background will need and value a guide in this new land. Others may, for some reason, feel they do not belong. Help them to find the one who makes yokes easy and makes burdens light; Jesus shared a meal with anyone.

Finally, find a consultant. Your teammates are informal consultants; yet nothing replaces a trained consultant who knows how to work for change and how to guide others in change. Review regularly what is happening and what might come next.

Helping people to change

Sometimes the change needs to occur in the missionary. Recall Kit who needed to take time for herself. George needed to speak up. Sometimes the change needs to occur in the others. Margaret needed to help Esther to change. Jim needed to help his family to be more peaceful. Insights about feedback and change can help the missionaries to work through the changes they need to make in themselves.

"Feedback" helps

One way to change one's own behavior is through something trainers in human relations call "feedback." (The following material is drawn from resources prepared by George L. Peabody and by Eleanor Hillers of Fayetteville, New York, consultants for churches and secular groups.) "Feedback," a space age term, refers to the data fed back to a missile to keep it on course. As people pursue their goals, they need "feedback" on how others are perceiving them as they work. Remember: other people act on the basis of how they perceive your behavior. What you intend and what the other perceives are not always the same.

Feedback comes in many forms: actions like a nod of the head, leaving a room, words of thanks or resistance. If the feedback is not flowing, ask for it: ask anything from "Does this make sense?" to "How am I coming across to you?" If it is confusing, ask for clarification. And be sure to get it from several people. Different people will perceive your actions differently. Here are some things to keep in mind:

- The perceiver is the authority. Do not argue, defend, or explain. Interrupt only to get clear on what the perceiver is saying to you.

- Get feedback from several people. There is no "immaculate perception." One's own perception is limited. You need the help of the others.

- Tactfully, help the giver to follow the "rules" for giving feedback (see below).

- Keep your thoughts about the feedback to yourself. Recall the "yep, nope, maybe" rule. If — "yep" — you agree, welcome it. If — "nope" — you disagree, say "maybe" and think about it for two weeks. It may become "yep." If it is still "nope," dismiss it.

- After the feedback is given, feel free to ask how you might have been more effective.

- Say "thanks" for the feedback. If you don't acknowledge the feedback, you may discourage further gifts. Responsible feedback is a gift.

To help others work with you effectively, you will need to learn to give feedback responsibly. When you do, try to follow these guideposts:

- Remember, feedback is a mirror, not a directive. The receiver controls using it or not using it;
- Give feedback as close to the event as you possibly can;
- Be specific. Name the specific words or actions that you are going to talk about;
- Talk about just that word or action and say how you perceived it. Also talk about its impact on others or on the task as you perceived it;
- Be sure what you say is worded so that the other person can "hear" and use it. Include how the person can help you or be more effective the next time;
- Ask other people to share with you how they perceived the same words or actions.

Feedback has three forms:

1. Leveling: feedback's usual form, occurs when you tell the other how you are perceiving the other person's words or actions. It is about you, yourself.

2. Confronting: telling the other person or persons how you feel or think about them. It is about them. Margaret confronts Esther when she says that she perceives Esther to be afraid of her.

3. Encounter: free exchange and dialogue both ways. Each gives and receives. Each is open to change. Margaret and Esther seem to be working toward a relationship of ongoing encounter.

George Peabody says about feedback: "The genius of it is not the information you give and receive, but the experience of telling the truth to each other. It helps you begin to take responsibility for your own actions."

Put all this about feedback together in two steps and it becomes easier to practice.

1. Behavior: Identify the specific behavior — what was said or done.

2. Perception: Say how you saw or felt about the behavior; ask others how they saw it.

Learning new skills

Some of the ways in learning to do new things have been outlined by Matthew Miles (*Learning to Work in Groups*, Columbia University, 1959), an early writer in human relations. A companion who walks beside the partner during these six steps can make the path much easier to follow.

1. The learner becomes dissatisfied with the way he or she is doing something;

2. The learner looks for, finds, and chooses some new way to learn to act. The companion helps by sharing his or her own constant need for change and by widening the range of options from which to choose. This step is similar to Question #4 for discerning one of your missions;

3. The learner practices these new options. Since the learner is quite vulnerable during this practice, the companion offers strong emotional support and encouragement;

4. The learner receives feedback from other people on the practice. The learner keeps practicing the various options, until one or more ways that work are found. The companion helps the learner to follow the guides for receiving feedback noted above;

5. The learner reflects on what works, connects it with past experience, and begins to make it part of his or her actions from that point on. The companion continues to give support and encouragement;

6. The learner faces new problems and new dissatisfactions arise. Walking the six steps continues and the companion remains available.

Two diagrams adapted from Miles can help the missionary to remember these steps and their constant repetition (see Figure 6, p. 160).

Helping systems to change

The changes missionaries believe they are called to make will, often, be changes in what we have come to call "systems." We are surrounded by systems. A system is any group of people who work together to achieve a purpose they hold in common. Organizations, corporations, unions, congregations, and even families are systems. Some are gigantic like the United States government. Some are quite small like a prayer group. Some are subsystems that make up a larger system. Eddie works to change a subsystem, his practice group at the firm. Gloria works to change a massive system, that branch of education that teaches mathematics. Three

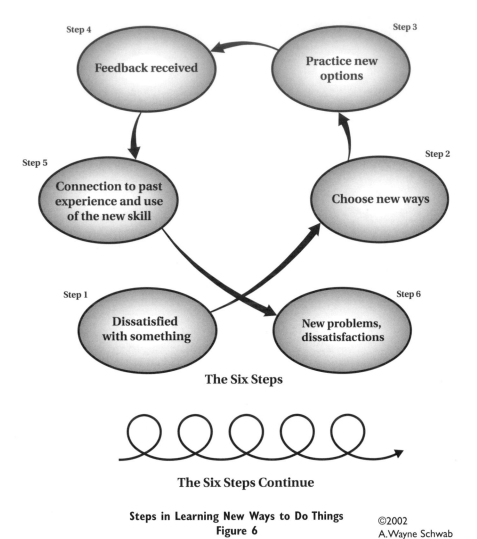

Step 4
Feedback received

Step 3
Practice new options

Step 5
Connection to past experience and use of the new skill

Step 2
Choose new ways

Step 1
Dissatisfied with something

Step 6
New problems, dissatisfactions

The Six Steps

The Six Steps Continue

**Steps in Learning New Ways to Do Things
Figure 6**

©2002
A. Wayne Schwab

comments on systems may help the missionaries as they contemplate needed changes in systems.

First, defective systems are often the cause of defective behavior. Changing the system often improves the behavior of the people in it. Remember Susan's story — she works to change the system of home ownership in low-income neighborhoods. As residents are taught how to care for their own homes they experience success they had not known before. Sometimes, a missionary will create a new system to counter an existing problem system. Robbie created a group to foster spirituality among Indian youths; "Strong Heart" will counter the negative influence of a culture that does not appreciate the religious insight of Indian people. He is building a new system within the problem-creating system of the dominant Anglo-culture.

Second, systems often have habits that the people in them do not recognize. These habits — or norms — are discovered when someone does something contrary to them. The norm breaker experiences disapproval. As he reflects on what brought on the disapproval, he may discern the norm he must have broken. Can long-existing norms be changed? They can! Change is not that difficult. Just point out the norm in so many words. "It looks as if the last thing anyone around here can do is say what they think." Once a hidden norm is spotted and pointed out for all to see, it usually begins to lose its power to influence behavior. The moment George, who was trying to change the norm of not speaking up, spoke up, things began to change at the post office. When Leila links Don's need for time off with her own need for time off, she questions a hidden norm of no time off. Time off for both becomes the new norm.

Third, while costly publications, seminars, and consulting firms for changing systems abound, following the seven steps to discern your mission in a given arena can be enough to bring about change. The storytellers of Part 1 had not read a raft of books and gone to a year of conferences for change agents. Their visions were clear and they were fed the power to act on them. God worked with and through them for change.

You may find it interesting to see how change in systems parallels the way people learn a new skill. Following are steps drawn from presentations at various church and group life laboratories sponsored by the Episcopal Church as early as the 1950s and sixties. A favored guide was an early book in the field, *The Dynamics of Planned Change* (Harcourt, Brace & World, 1958), by Ronald Lippitt, Jeanne Watson, and Bruce Westley. Its simplicity gives it lasting value:

- Recognize the need for change.

- Look for a helper who will consult with you as you go. Find a friend whom you trust to tell the truth, even when the truth may be hard to take.

- Diagnose the problem and choose what to change. This step is similar to Questions #3 and #4 for discerning one of your missions.

- Start the change.

- Collect information on how the change is going and modify direction as needed.

- Reflect on what has happened and change the way things are done from now on.

- Be ready to see what needs change or improvement next.

For further reading

To explore systemic change further, here are some more current resources I have found useful for work with congregations changing to a vision of the members as the missionaries.

Walter Wink, *The Powers That Be: Theology for a New Millennium* (Galilee, 1998). Wink offers a theology to undergird work in changing systems. He summarizes his earlier trilogy of *Naming the Powers: The Language of Power in the New Testament* (Fortress, 1984); *Unmasking the Powers: The Invisible Forces That Determine Human Existence* (Fortress, 1986); and *Engaging the Powers: Discernment and Resistance in a World of Domination* (Fortress, 1992).

Max DePree, *Leadership is an Art* (Dell, 1989). DePree describes how he made changes as chairman and CEO of Herman Miller, Inc., a furniture maker. Milton Moskowitz, in "The One Hundred Best Companies to Work for in America" (Addison, Wesley, 1984), named it among those top companies. In 1986, a *Fortune* poll picked it as one of the nation's "ten most admired companies" for "quality of products or services."

Peter M. Senge, *The Fifth Discipline: The Art & Practice of The Learning Organization* (Currency, 1990). Organizations must discover how to tap people's commitment and capacity to learn at all levels of the organization. Five disciplines must work together — systems thinking, personal mastery, surfacing and challenging mental models, building shared vision, and team learning. Systems thinking is the glue that binds the other four disciplines together and makes them all work.

Ron Lippitt is an applied behavioral scientist who originated theories that have shaped the field of organization development or OD. He found that when he asked people to develop shared solutions to their problems, he drained their energy and raised blaming. When he asked, "What do you want to be like in five years when you are working at your best?" he found all the participants were energized. (See Robert Jacobs' *Real Time Strategic Change*, Berrett-Koehler, 1994, for more on large group visioning.)

Barbara Bunker and Billie Alban, *Large Group Interventions: Engaging the Whole System for Rapid Change* (Jossey-Bass, 1996). Bunker and Alban review the several methods for bringing large groups — hundreds at a time — of people together: to develop a vision and plan for the future; to explore issues and to problem solve; and to work in the design or redesign of an organization or of business processes. They give an overview of procedures for each purpose, their developers, and their publications. The principle is to get all the people concerned about a problem together at one time. Because they are the key people, their decisions become the change being sought. Church leaders reorienting their congregation around the members as the missionaries will want to look into the resources in the section of the book on visioning and planning.

The Harvard Business Review. Review the last two years under the topic "change."

Jerry B. Harvey, *The Abilene Paradox and Other Meditations on Management* (Jossey-Bass, 1996 edition). A professor of management science at George Washington University in Washington, D.C., Harvey has produced a number of unconventional and thought-provoking views about groups and systems. On encouraging difference of opinion, he comments, "It is my contention that the inability to cope with (manage) agreement, rather than the inability to cope with (manage) conflict, is the single most pressing issue of modern organizations. (p. 17)" Elsewhere, he tells of the Japan Air Lines pilot who landed his jet in San Francisco Bay two and a half miles short of the runway. The first question put to the pilot, Captain Kohei Asoh, at the hearing was how did he "manage" to do that. Virtually ending the hearing, he answered, "As you Americans say, Asoh [messed] up. (p. 63)" Harvey observes that Asoh not only fed those starving for truth in the corporate world, but took responsibility for his own actions and opened up the chance for patterns of forgiveness. Freedom to disagree, telling the truth, taking responsibility, and forgiveness are essential to support the members as missionaries. ✦

Chapter 15 — Some Specifics About Small Groups

Along with worship, support for the missionary is best provided through biblical reflection in small groups. Numbering from two to six, the groups meet at least biweekly in the members' homes. Do not make where people live the primary guide for choosing members of a group. Assemble groups based on the members' readiness and desire to work together. Affinity is a better guide than geography. A group just finishing preparation for baptism or reaffirmation is a natural group.

The general content of reflection is always what does this biblical passage say and what does it say to me for the week or two ahead. Put biblical insight together with daily living. Keep in mind that no one participant is the expert. The Holy Spirit is the real leader. Unusual readings by one are usually balanced by the wisdom of the rest.

This linking of the Bible and daily life was a basic part of the catechumenal process of the early church according to Louis Weil, Hodges Professor of Liturgy at the Church Divinity School of the Pacific in Berkeley, California. It has ebbed and flowed in use throughout church history. In our time, its practice has grown steadily since the 1950s. For an overview of various methods, see *In Dialogue With Scripture*, The Episcopal Church Center, 1992. Each method has a unique way to connect the passage and daily life. Ideally, some form of biblical reflection on daily life is part of every church meeting.

A widely used form for biblical reflection

A form of biblical reflection widely used follows. Built around three readings of the passage with a specific reflection after each reading, it it is often called simply the "oral" method. It makes all the participants peers and it connects with their daily lives easily. Directions for its use follow. Some congregations have built their whole catechumenate around this method (adapted from *In Dialog with Scripture*). Youth can work easily in groups using it. The simple format makes it easy to rotate leadership.

Step 1. Each person shares his or her experience in the area of prayer from the previous session. (If this is the first session, begin with Step 2.)

Step 2. Read the passage slowly (one person reads out loud).

Step 3. In a period of silence, select the word or phrase that catches your attention (one minute).

Step 4. Each person shares the word or phrase with the group.

Step 5. Read the passage again (opposite gender of first reader, if possible).

Step 6. In a period of silence, think out/write: "Where does this passage touch my life, my community, our nation, or our world? Think about all the people you encounter, not just your own 'circle of friends.' Think also of all whose lives you influence even though you never see them." (3-5 minutes).

Step 7. Each person shares the above: "I . . . "

Step 8. Read the passage out loud again.

Step 9. Think out/write: "From what I have heard and shared, what does God want me to do or be this week? How does God invite me to change?" (3-5 minutes).

Step 10. Each person shares the above: "I . . . "

Step 11. Each person prays for the person on the right naming what was shared in #10 and then prays that prayer daily until the group meets again.

Some things to note when using this method:

• What is said is offered to the "center" of the group — the Holy Spirit. Others do not respond to or build on what is said as if they were in a discussion group.

• In Steps 3, 7, and 10, be brief. Do not elaborate, explain, or teach.

• In Step 6, be sure to name all the contexts each time — your life, your community, our nation, and our world; and all people, even those whose lives we affect but whom we never see.

• Assure all members that they can pass any time they do not want to share or are not ready to share. Assure all members that, at the prayer time, they can pray silently for the person on their right and say only "Amen" aloud.

In whatever method is used, conclude the session with each person making a specific prayer request arising from the reflection just completed. When the oral method is used, responses to the third question (see Steps 10 and 11) become the basis for these prayers. All then pray for the person on their right and pray that prayer daily until the next meeting. As the next session begins, each names the specific prayer offered since the last session. The person prayed for responds with a report of what has happened since the last session in the concern prayed for. Very often, this person is surprised to discern answers to the prayer he or she had missed until asked. This surprise brings a unique sense of God's presence and work in one's life.

Another place the Spirit speaks is the prayer request time itself. Sometimes another person sees something the requester has not seen. Once Tom, a personnel director, asked prayer for guidance in a career change. Another person in the group recalled that Tom had told the group earlier that many were coming to his office for help in solving conflicts. The member suggested Tom explore conflict resolution as a career option. Tom welcomed the suggestion and reported later it had led to wholly new areas of work for him.

Biblical reflection of this kind bears rich fruit. Invariably, it increases the confidence of the laity to talk freely of God and God's work in their lives. One woman remarked that it was the first time in her life that she had been treated on a par with men. Several men commented that her reflections opened them to new awareness. A man said, "We have developed a closeness I never expected. It is so good to hear us pray for each other. We discover we can be deep, spiritual, friendly, and human all at once." Another person said, "We are learning to respect each other's opinions. We don't have to agree on everything and we don't have to persuade each other of our own views." Another person observed, "It is an easy way to learn how to lead small groups." Another said, "My sense of being on mission has increased each time." ✦

Chapter 16 — How Worship and Preaching Can Nurture the Vision

The vision in worship

The connection between Sunday worship and Monday to Saturday living is hardly new. Frank T. Griswold III, Presiding Bishop of the Episcopal Church, recalled this at some length in the Zabriskie Lecture at Virginia Theological Seminary in October 1999. Griswold told of George Herbert ringing the church bell and saying Matins and Evensong in the small rural town of Bemerton in seventeenth century England. Griswold recalled, "The towns people and the farmers nearby, when they heard the bell, would stop because they knew he [Herbert] was at his prayers and would join themselves to him in prayer." From this century of the liturgical movement, Griswold noted the work of A. G. Hebert, writer and teacher of liturgical theology, on the bond between worship and life. Griswold commented, "It is very clear if you . . . read Hebert's book, *Liturgy and Society* (1935), that liturgy is profoundly connected to the life people live, and that was another profound concern of the shapers and framers of the liturgical movement."

As the baptized grow in understanding mission, they begin to pray about the arenas of daily life as they come to see them as their mission fields. Increasingly, they come to corporate worship for direction and power for living in those daily arenas.

Planning worship

While control of worship is given to the clergy, wise clergy share that control with a team of worship planners. Such a team can ask members if each word and each action of worship affirm, express, or enable the lives of the members in their mission fields. The team listens with one ear to tradition and with one ear to today's world — its needs and "language." Associated Parishes for Liturgy and Mission (Associated Parishes, PO Box 27141, Baltimore, Maryland 21230-0141) offers useful guides for beginners in worship planning. While these guides may not have a full vision of the laity as missionaries, they will get you started.

Six principles can guide the planning of worship that recognizes the missions of the worshipers. Three general principles are:

1. Liturgy should express the way we live rather than be a separate exercise apart from life.

2. The connections between the liturgy and real life should be easy to discern.

3. Adapt the worship to the specific characteristics of the place of the worship.

Three specific principles are:

1. Find ways to express the specific daily missions of the worshipers.

2. Find ways for the laity to share their own journeys in faith during worship.

3. Make sure the laity are prominent and visible in leading worship in order to demonstrate their mission in church life.

The following examples illustrate these principles.

Making changes in worship

The pastor and the people of Trinity Church, Asbury Park, New Jersey, have a useful story to tell about making changes in worship that connect daily life and worship. Apparently, they saw using inclusive language as a way to affirm equal participation in mission by all of the members. They used this procedure to introduce it:

> We never ask people to reflect on new material, until they have experienced it for a number of months. We had the vestry's consent to work this way. We said, "This is a new set of liturgical prayers [Supplemental Liturgical Texts, Prayer Book Studies 30, Church Publishing, Inc., with its inclusive language] approved by General Convention for trial use. We would like to try them and see what you think about them." After about three months of using one of them, we discussed it — and it was almost universally popular. We had not talked about the philosophy of inclusion in these texts when we introduced them. It would not have made sense until there was some idea of what it was about by actually using it. This is liturgy, not just a book. It has to be lived out before people can sincerely reflect on it with more than a knee-jerk reaction. The overwhelming result was that these are now our principal texts — especially, the second

eucharistic prayer which works well with gestures at the altar (one thing you will never see by reading it only) — from the specifics of the bread to prayer for the Spirit [to brood] over the whole world.

Trinity Church has used this same procedure to introduce oral Bible study and dialogue sermons as regular parts of Sunday worship. This pattern can also be used for changing the placement of furniture in a church. For example, placing the baptismal font in the center aisle is a small town church's way to remind worshipers every Sunday that they have joined the mission of God's reign in Jesus Christ.

Baptism and Easter

Make sure that baptism and the celebration of Easter are about living the mission. Critique everything from the preparation of adults and parents and godparents to the place and size of the font and the content of the sermon at baptism. Because the core celebration of the year is the Easter Vigil, give some thought to the selection of readings, to their length, and to the manner of reading. Include readings from the prophets. Three hours after dark on Easter Eve may not be the best time for maximum congregational participation. A combination of pantomime and speaking parts done by children of the congregation can help worshipers to connect the readings with today's world. Further, remember "Sundays are little Easters." Make sure Sunday worship frequently expresses joining the mission in baptism. Associated Parishes, among other resources, can help the planners find their way in both the Vigil and each Sunday's worship. Consult the web site of the North American Association for the Catechumenate (www.catechumenate.org) as another resource for planning. In all, make sure that baptism and the celebration of Easter express belief that baptism is joining the mission and being empowered for it.

Preaching for and by missionaries

The missionaries should share in the planning and evaluation of preaching. When James R. Adams was the rector of St. Mark's Church, Capitol Hill, Washington, D.C., a liturgy planning group read the lections for Sunday and shared their thoughts and questions about them with the preacher for the day. For feedback at a pastoral size church, three people taped their answers to: "What did the preacher say?" "What did you think of what the preacher said?" and "What do you want to say to preachers in general?" At a family size church, the preacher simply asks one or two after the worship. "How did that sermon work for you?"

Sermons for missionaries seem to need, at least, one story of a missionary in one of the daily arenas. It helps when the story includes any or all of the following: what was blocking God's work, what was done, how God was talked about, and the results. When the power of God — of God's reign among us — comes through the story clearly, mission has been demonstrated.

In some congregations, the missionaries tell their own stories as part of the sermon. The priest follows the sharing with a brief teaching. At Trinity Church, Asbury Park, New Jersey, the people taught the sacraments during Eastertide at sermon time. They described what baptism and the eucharist meant to them. The pastor summarized their talks and did some teaching. At the Good Friday liturgy at Grace Church, Canton, New York, a teacher, a business person, and a nurse spoke. They told about how they once felt hopeless in their work, how they gave it all up to God, and how they felt afterward. They also shared what happened to the people around them as a result of giving their situations up to God.

The missionaries do the interceding and thanksgiving

In the Episcopal eucharist, the Prayers of the People are too often not offered by the people but by readers "up front." Form VI has the clearest openings for each missionary to offer his or her own prayers. Vary the other five forms to invite the people's prayers and thanksgivings. Allow time for those who collect their thoughts slowly to join in. If needed, count to ten after the last audible prayer before saying the next words. One practice is to give the reader the task of offering specific prayers for the local community and wider world if none are offered by the congregation.

Shaping worship around the missionaries

Weddings can express the mission of the laity in home and marriage. An Episcopal parson in a Northeastern state made imaginative variations for the wedding of a couple with grown children who had families of their own. They follow in note form.

- Before the rite started, the minister briefed the congregation about their responsibility to support the couple as part of their mission to the new home being created. Then, he focused his remarks by practice of a hearty response to the question, "Will all of you witnessing these promises do all within your power to uphold these two persons in their marriage?" (See the *Book of Common Prayer*, p. 425.)

- The bride and groom processed to the front side by side. The wedding party followed. Thus, they demonstrated their own responsibility to make the marriage work.

- The bride and groom were seated side by side facing the congregation and in the center. The parson was at the side and stayed there when he rose to speak. This seating suggested that the primary ministers of the marriage were the bride and the groom.

- During the exchange of the vows, the couple stood facing each other with the clergy, maid of honor, and best man at the side as the only witnesses. Prompting for the vows came from the best man and maid of honor.

- After they were pronounced husband and wife, the couple introduced their sons and daughters and their families to the congregation.

This same parson developed ways to express the mission of the members at funerals. He planned a lot of participation by the family and friends in the burial liturgy — e.g., reading, leading the psalms, and sharing in litany forms. Central to the sharing was preparing the funeral sermon with the family. To plan a recent funeral, the priest asked the family to share "stories — humorous and otherwise — of [their] mom's gifts to [them]." They told about their mother's generosity to the hungry, her unconditional love for each of them, her skill in nursing others through illness, and her justice and fairness. In the homily at the funeral, he called what this woman did the work of a missionary and affirmed that she was surely one of God's co-workers.

The same minister tells of a memorial eucharist held in a funeral home. The deceased person had been one of the three remaining active members of an Episcopal congregation in a small town in upstate New York when it was closed. The priest rearranged the seating to express the active mission of the laity, prepared the family to share in a way that expressed the missions of the deceased person, and provided an order of service that did the same. The family and friends affirmed their appreciation for the approach. He describes the eucharist as follows.

Because of difficult travel logistics, I was not able to meet with the family before the memorial eucharist at the funeral home. The funeral director had set up the room with the casket in the front and rows of chairs facing forward. We changed the seating by putting the chairs in a three-sided arrangement, with a small communion table in front of the casket on the fourth side. While waiting for others to arrive, the family, friends, and I met in the anteroom of the funeral home and talked about the life of the deceased person. I had relatives read the lections. After a short homily on the subject of feasting together contrasted with judging alone, I asked each person to say something that they were thankful for in the life of the deceased. In place of the usual preface to the Eucharistic prayer, I incorporated the thanksgivings for the deceased person that had been mentioned during the sharing time. All were encouraged to receive communion, regardless of age or denominational background.

Here is another example of how a funeral observance can be designed around the missionary. A young psychiatric nurse and member of St. Brendan's Church, Juneau, Alaska, died suddenly. A counselor at a community health agency, she was much appreciated by her clients and co-workers. Because some of her clients would not feel comfortable in "church," members of St. Brendan's on her staff held a second gathering away from the church. The nurse's clients and co-workers gathered at her work site and shared informally with her husband, son, and parents appreciative stories about her. Also, since she and her husband were members of The Society of Creative Anachronisms dedicated to celebrating the Middle Ages "as they should have been," some of their SCA friends wore medieval costumes to her burial service at the church. They were celebrating one of her leisure time missions.

In still another direction, Christians, since apostolic times, have used the native language of the people they serve as a bridge to the Christian Gospel, worship and life. Worship in the language of the people connects with the people's mission in the wider world of their culture. In this tradition, an Ojibwa lay catechist leads a group in Bemidji, Minnesota, that meets twice a month for Gospel Based Discipleship using the Ojibwa language. This linking of Jesus and their daily lives with its reflection, prayer, and action is their worship for the time being. The 17 - 24 adult and teen participants find they "fit" in this kind of Episcopal setting. Gospel Based Discipleship (see p. 94) in Ojibwa is also the medium for this lay catechist to gather an average of sixteen children from four to thirteen years old at St. John's Church on the Red Lake Reservation where she lives. She introduces herself as "grandmother at church" drawing on the family values of Indian culture. This is their form of worship for the time being also. ✦

Chapter 17 — The Kind of Leaders This Vision Needs

What kind of leaders do congregations need to help them to set up the various parts of their common vision and to make them work? Congregations need leaders, not managers.

A breakthrough in leadership theory came in 1977 when Abraham Zaleznik published an article in the *Harvard Business Review*. Zaleznik is Konosuke Matsushita Professor of Leadership Emeritus at Harvard Business School, one of the few certified psychoanalysts in the United States without a medical degree, and the author of fourteen books and numerous articles. In his article, he distinguished between leaders and managers: managers make what is work better and leaders make what is into something new. His observations shed light on the kind of people congregations need as leaders to organize around the missions of the members. (See "Managers and Leaders: Are They Different?" *Harvard Business Review*, May-June 1977.)

Zaleznik begins by quoting John D. Rockefeller III on the conservatism of organizations: "An organization is a system, with a logic of its own, and all the weight of tradition and inertia. The deck is stacked in favor of the tried and proven way of doing things and against the taking of risks and striking out in new directions." Zaleznik continues, "Out of this conservatism and inertia, organizations provide succession to power through the development of managers rather than individual leaders. Ironically, this ethic fosters a bureaucratic culture in business, supposedly the last bastion protecting us from the encroachments and controls of bureaucracy in government and education."

The distinctions in his article can be charted as follows.

Leaders vs Managers

Vision vs Order

"Vision, the hallmark of leadership, is less a derivative of spreadsheets and more a product of the mind called imagination. And vision is needed at least as much as strategy to succeed . . . . A leader's imagination impels others to act in ways that are truly, to use James MacGregor Burns's felicitous term, 'transformational.'"

"Managers are almost compulsively addicted to disposing of problems, even before they understand their potential significance. In my experience, seldom do the uncertainties of potential chaos cause problems. Instead, it is the instinctive move to impose order on potential chaos that makes trouble for organizations"

Goal-setting vs Problem-solving

" . . . leaders think about goals. They are active instead of reactive, shaping ideas instead of responding to them."

"A managerial culture emphasizes rationality and control . . . a manager is a problem solver."

Change vs Preservation

"The methods [leaders use] to bring about change may be technological, political, or ideological, but the object is the same: to profoundly alter human, economic and political relationships."

"A manager's sense of self-worth is enhanced by perpetuating and strengthening existing institutions . . . ."

Risk vs Balance

"Where managers act to limit choices, leaders develop fresh approaches to long-standing problems and open issues to new options. To be effective, leaders must project their ideas onto images that excite people and only then develop choices that give those images substance. Leaders sometimes react to mundane work as to an affliction."

"To get people to accept solutions to problems, managers continually need to balance opposing views . . . . Managers aim to shift balances of power toward solutions acceptable as compromises among conflicting values . . . . For those who become managers, a survival instinct dominates the need for risk, and with that instinct comes an ability to tolerate mundane, practical work."

Assertive vs Congenial Climate

"I wonder whether a greater capacity in senior officers to tolerate the competitive impulses and behavior of their subordinates might not be healthy for corporations."

"A chief executive officer naturally has the right to select people with whom he feels congenial."

Zaleznik's work stimulates rethinking the role of clergy in church life. Leaders need to manage and managers need to lead. However, when a congregation moves toward the vision of the member as the missionary, the leader role is needed over the manager role. Constant dialogue about the vision will call for vigorous advocacy for the vision from the leader. On the one hand, the leader will override no one. On the other hand, leaders are free to articulate visions that include their own convictions.

The role of the ordained as leader

"Leader" appears little in the New Testament. However, the image of the shepherd leading his flock has a central place. "Pastor" is a much used synonym for "shepherd." "Pastor" is one of the chief words used in ordaining bishops and priests in the Episcopal *Book of Common Prayer*. In many communions, the ordained person is addressed as "pastor." When we talk of pastoring, we are, in part, talking of leadership. Therefore, to bring secular insight into clerical leadership is fitting.

The Rt. Rev. J. M. Mark Dyer offered these theological reflections on leadership in a recent conversation. The retired Episcopal bishop of Bethlehem, he is Professor of Theology and Director of Spiritual Formation at the Virginia Theological Seminary and Anglican Co-chair of the International Commission of the Anglican-Orthodox Theological Dialogue.

- Leadership is one of the gifts of the Holy Spirit.

- Jesus Christ is the leader. All leadership is derived from his leadership.

- We do not own leadership. Our task is to keep learning about it.

- The Holy Spirit works among us keeping our learning about leadership an ongoing process.

What follows is part of that ongoing process of learning about leadership. The role of the clergy is heightened in vitality when they lead in the move away from making what is work better toward making what is into something new. Their role is not diminished as some fear. The crucial functions of clergy leaders are daunting:

- Teach that mission is primary and that the church is the visible presence of Christ in the world.

- Lead in the recovery of corporate worship as the work of the whole people of God and share responsibility for the planning and leading of liturgy with the members.

- Hold up the vision of every baptized person as a missionary.

- Develop the members' desire to realize the vision.

- Recruit members to lead in moving toward this vision and provide for their training in their new role.

- Help the leaders form a team to organize themselves to plan how the vision will take on flesh.

- Support the leaders as they organize the congregation for training for mission by:

   providing some kind of catechumenal formation to form newcomers as conscious agents of mission;

   providing all members the Christian survival skills of common and individual prayer, theological reflection, Christian decision making in both personal and social concerns, and how to work with others for change; and

   providing access to regional and ecumenical events where training for mission is provided that is beyond the scope of their own congregation to provide.

- Support the forming of affinity-based small groups for biblical reflection and mutual support for ministry in daily life.

- Support the mission of the congregation as a body in its mission to its community — beginning with ministry with the poor.

- Foster the communication needed for people to move from the old vision of the priest as the primary missionary and mission leader to the new vision of each member as a missionary.

- Advocate for the new vision at all times.

- Pursue constantly one's own physical, emotional, and spiritual health.

To carry on these functions, the leader needs skills. Leading from what is into something new takes all the group process skills a leader can muster. Too many claim they know group process, when they really do not. Do not assume you have learned group process by auditing some lectures or by taking the Myers-Briggs Type Indicator®. Adequate training in process calls for the experience of an unstructured training group of eight to twelve with a skilled trainer and observer. Further, the sessions should be two to three hours per day for a week and two weeks is better. While much of church work is done in much larger groups, many of the group process skills needed for large group work are best learned in a small group.

To be even more specific, learn good group behavior with this application of the steps in personal change from pages 157-160.

1. Do something with a group — for example, practice chairing a fifteen-minute or so meeting.

2. Get feedback on your own behavior from a trained observer and from the rest of the group.

3. Draw out your learnings from how others perceived you and formulate some new behavior to try.

4. Try it in the same kind of fifteen-minute session.

5. Get further feedback on your behavior in that session.

6. Either save and build on the pattern or try a new one — repeating these same steps.

Asking for feedback, receiving it, and learning from it are probably the most basic group process skills of all. Right after it comes learning to give feedback. Such training is hard to find. NTL Institute for Applied Behavioral Science (1-800-777-5227; www.ntl.org) training can be costly. Look around for universities that offer experiential training that includes practice, feedback, and repractice. You may know of a process-trained person who can help you on a minimum basis — e.g., observe a two-hour meeting and then spend an hour with you looking at and learning from the process of that meeting. Also, practice the skills of giving and receiving feedback (see pp. 157-158) on your own.

Leading from what is into something new also takes all the communication skills a leader can muster. Communication skills are easier to learn — in some ways — than group process skills. However, you will learn communication skills more easily, if you are getting or have gotten some process training already. As in group process training, you need to practice, get feedback, and repractice. Do not assume you have learned communication skills in an Andrew Carnegie course. The issue is two-way communication, not public speaking.

This "communication age" misleads us. What is meant to connect, usually alienates. The so-called "media" of television, radio, and print lack two-way communication. The listener or reader has no way to respond. E-mail tempts us to assume that sending and receiving messages quickly is communication. We do not seem to realize that what a speaker intends to communicate may not be perceived accurately by the listener. E-mail is full of strong reactions without checking that what was perceived by one is what the other intended to communicate. The telephone does provide tone of voice. Being face-to-face offers communication its best chance. Some say 70 percent of communication is nonverbal. Face-to-face, I get to see your body language and gestures. Further, I can check that what I thought you said is what you meant to say. This patient checking is indispensable.

Seminaries and those interviewing their graduates

This vision of the members as the missionaries requires different leadership skills in the ordained than the old vision of "body-mission" — mission carried on by what the members do in church-sponsored programs and activities. Seminaries tend to train their students in leadership skills suited to the old vision. Members of faculties, members of boards of trustees and directors, and members of denominational agencies supporting seminaries who are imaginative and resolute can begin to raise questions about what vision of mission are we training students for. Interviewers of students in congregations and dioceses need to begin to ask themselves what their own vision of mission is. Sensitive faculty and church leaders tend to find that most interviewers ask questions based on a vision of the suburban church of the 1950s. It is time to ask interviewees about who they believe carries on the mission of Jesus Christ today and how will they support them in their missions. While change is always possible, its seekers must be intentional and willing to labor without ceasing.

An overview of the "path" we follow

A congregation is "designed" to get the results it is getting.

If we do not change the vision of the congregation's purpose, we will continue to get what we have always gotten.

If we embrace a new vision, we must redesign the congregation around it.

Every member and every leader need to understand and do their part to realize the vision.

If we all make the hard day-by-day decisions to implement the new vision for ten years, we will begin to see results.

For God's "pathfinders"

Work as if everything depends on you. Pray as if everything depends on God. ✦

Chapter 18 — Going on from Here

Moving from the priest as the missionary to the members as the missionaries takes, at least, ten years to get started. It is like turning around a large tanker at sea. The tanker turns very slowly over a course that is miles long. Long-term change with a group of people calls for a lot of negotiation and compromise. Group process and communication skills help you to negotiate and to compromise.

All the missionaries in congregations need the same skills. The clergy leader needs skill as a trainer. Much of the clergy leader's training is done indirectly through modeling the desired behavior. Direct training by the leader is likely to be minimal. Clergy leaders, rather, use their skill as trainers to diagnose what skills are needed, find ways for members to learn them, and support the members and the actual leader of the training while it is under way.

Building a loving and just congregation

To paraphrase Paul, "If I have all the skills in the world and the ability to train others in them, but am not loving and just, I am still part of the problem, not the solution" (1 Corinthians 13:1). A loving and just — or fair — leader is the best builder of a loving and just congregation.

Practice of these skills and insights by leaders, both clergy and lay, will do a lot to build loving and just congregations.

Lack of skills in group process, feedback, communication, negotiation, compromise, and training others often blocks growth in love and justice. While these are not the only skills needed, it is hard to lead without them.

Leaders need ongoing access to a competent consultant with whom to review their work step-by-step and to keep sharpening their skills and insights as leaders.

Throughout, both leaders and congregation need the Holy Spirit. Love and justice, wherever they are found, are the gift and work of the Holy Spirit. When Spirit-led, the caring and fairness of congregations and their members become the most contagious when lived out in the daily arenas of the members.

Finding your own support

Leadership is lonely. Leading others into a new vision of how to believe and how to live compounds the loneliness. Loneliness can inhibit growth. Overcome being alone by building a network of support. People are the primary supports. Do not expect the key lay leaders of the congregation or the clergy of the church next door or the diocese to understand, much less share, your vision. Rather, find others who can understand the vision. Still more, find others who are willing to help you to realize it. Then, keep in touch with them in whatever you do.

Develop your skills for dialogue. Welcome far out — even contradictory — views. When they come, listen with care to be sure you understand them. Then respond with candor. Constantly, practice and talk of our need to live lovingly and justly all the time. Who can deny that we need to find some way to work harder at making that happen? We seldom hear, "See how these Christians are always in the forefront of more loving and just living?" Genuine dialogue often leads to discovering some unexpected support.

Do not expect your regional or national leaders to grasp and to support your work. They are probably caught in the system you are trying to change. In their presence, do not hold back from being clear about your vision. Accept that there is a slim chance they might want to hear more about it.

You may find decisive support in people from other communions. You may be surprised to find support in people from other religions. People you meet in wholly secular or nonchurch places can be your allies too.

Do look for training events related to the vision. You will find more allies and new ideas there. Resources can also be found in journals, periodicals, newspapers, and books.

This particular book is not a finished work. Others will finish it.

When your excitement turns into to a sense of heavy duty, turn to your team and your consultants for help.

Probably your happiest discovery of support will be found in the people in the congregation who welcome the vision as you begin to share it. Happier still will be the times when you hear them leading others into the vision. Even happier than that will be times someone at a congregational gathering says, "Who will join me in mission and prayer in/at. . . ?"

Get started and keep working to realize the vision. Do not be afraid to make mistakes. Admit they are mistakes when you make them.

The Spirit can teach you the skills you lack through those around you.

Use your own common sense. It takes courage to use it!

Never give up!

Never.

Never.

Never!

It is said that those last six words come from Winston Churchill. He was the graduation speaker at the school of his childhood and youth where he had just barely succeeded as a student. He went to the rostrum, said those words, and sat down. ✦

Chapter 19 — Postscript After September 11, 2001

The collapsing towers of the World Trade Center and the gaping hole in the Pentagon changed the world. In the midst of the change were thousands of missionaries carrying on their specific missions of caring and protecting — many of them consciously on God's mission, many of them unconsciously, but still used by God to heal. They were much of God's means of deliverance to a distressed world at that time. There are many stories to tell of deliverance in the midst of the tragedy.

There were crowds lining the streets to cheer the helpers who came as volunteers from all over New York and nearby states. As they drove the three hundred miles south from our towns upstate, the fire and rescue squads remembered the teams of police from New York City who had helped revive our towns after the ice storm of 1998. Some of those police were probably among the three hundred plus police and fire fighters who were victims of the destruction.

That day, September 11, my wife and I turned on "Good Morning America" about 2:40 p.m. in Heidleberg, Germany. We were horrified by what we saw. We were visiting our daughter's family where her U.S. Army husband is stationed. The next day, our daughter kept her children's appointment with the pediatrician at the base hospital. As she came out of the office, busloads of German high schoolers were outside the fence. One by one, each student came forward and placed a flower in the fence.

When we landed in New York ten days later, we saw miles of waiting trucks, waiting to be inspected before being allowed to enter the city.

Six weeks later, stories of the depth of the destruction and the depths of heroism keep coming through. For example, Dan Rather's "48 Hours" told of the seventy-four Port Authority workers, both men and women, whose job is the safety of those in the buildings. They were at their stations helping people to escape when the towers fell —still at their missions and now with God.

Military personnel are at risk around and in Afghanistan. One soldier sees her mission as making sure that the military is not run by people who want only to "waste the enemy." Another soldier on mission carries two quotes in his wallet. One comes from a speech John F. Kennedy was to have made in Dallas, Texas the day he was assassinated:

> We, in this country, in this generation, are by destiny, rather than by choice, the watchmen of the walls of world freedom. We ask, therefore, that we may be worthy of the power and the responsibility, that we may exercise our strength with wisdom and restraint, that we may achieve in our time and for all times the ancient vision of peace on earth, good will toward men. That must always be our goal and the righteousness of our call must always underlie our strength for as it was written long ago, "except the Lord keep the city, the watchmen waketh but in vain."

The soldier points out the word "destiny" to mean that the U.S. did not ask to be the world's super power. It was thrust upon us. And, the watchmen, the soldiers, do soldier in vain, if the Lord does not keep the city, the nation. The Lord keeps the city through what each one of us does to serve God's reign of caring and justice.

The second quote the soldier carries comes from George Orwell:

> We sleep safe in our beds, because rough men stand ready in the night to visit violence on those that would do us harm.

President Bush has said our objective is to bring to justice the doers of these awful deeds and the regimes of the nations that support them. Our role as Christians is surely to see that this remains our objective and that we do not fall victim to "war fever." Further, we must continue to pursue the rule of justice for all in this world and the end of poverty, the abuse of nature, and hungry children. A world with people who have nothing to lose is a dangerous world.

We are called to understand how the Arab world sees us and to make the corrections in ourselves that we can no longer avoid. Here at home, we need to provide for one another better than we do. Healthcare for all, help for the poor, and protection of the environment need more attention.

Now, more than ever, each of us must carry out our own missions in each of our daily arenas to the best of our ability, God being our helper.

Front and center are our missions in the wider world.

These missions begin with all of us keeping ourselves as well informed as we can and giving ourselves to honest and frank conversation with one another. Somewhere, the Federalist Papers from the late 1780s said the bedrock of a working democracy is the free exchange of private opinion. As the proverb puts it, "for evil to triumph, it takes only enough good people doing nothing."

We can no longer afford the luxury of a privatized spirituality. Today's spirituality must be a public spirituality — a spirituality that both critiques the political and social orders and works with them for their improvement .

For the changes we need to come to pass, we need more of us living out our particular missions in the mission of God. We are called to serve the kingdom, the reign of God in all of life.

May all of us undertake our missions constantly fed and strengthened by God's word and by the bread and the cup of the Lord Jesus Christ. ✦

Appendix A — The Questions for Each Mission Field

Hints for working with the questions

The six mission fields are not as obvious in meaning as might first appear. For clarity some examples of each field follow.

Home – parenting; friendships; relationships among the residents; maintenance of the place of bed and board

Work – whatever one is paid to do; home manager; one who gives his or her time in exchange for a service; school for students; volunteer work of the retiree or of the independently wealthy

Local community – soccer referee; elected town officer; school board member

Wider world – writing a letter about social issues to the editor of a national publication; participant in an environmental group; worker for a county, state, or national political party

Leisure – hobby; favorite recreation; care for our own physical or psychological health

Church – work as part of a congregation's food shelf; reader of biblical selections in worship; home visitor

The general pattern of the questions for each field follows accompanied by the assumptions that underlie each one. Use the alternate wording as desired. Copy these pages as needed.

1. What has God been telling me or doing through my life in this mission field?

   Assumption: God is already present and at work in each of one's mission fields.

2. What conditions inhibit reconciliation, justice, and love (peacemaking, fairness, and caring) in this mission field?

   Assumption: God's characteristic works are reconciliation, justice, and love. Hence, to begin to discern what God is already doing, look for what is blocking God's characteristic works. These will be the places where God is already working for change.

3. What change is needed to increase reconciliation, justice, and love (peacemaking, fairness, and caring) in this mission field?

   Assumption: The Holy Spirit works to align the Christian's discernment of what is needed with what God is already doing. This question draws on the unique being of each Christian. Two parents in the same home will probably discern different needed changes. Two workers in the same workplace will probably discern different needed changes.

4. What will I do to achieve this change considering my gifts, limitations, and convictions?

   Assumption: One draws on what one brings to the situation. While growth into some new direction may well be called for, that new direction will be a logical next step in the Christian's growth.

5. What vision (description of what I will do) will I use to draw others into working with me for this change?

   Assumption: The Christian needs at least one person, but preferably a team, to share the mission. The Christian's companion or team may not share the Christian faith so a vision should be worded in non-theological language and worded in a way that stimulates in others desire to work for it.

6. How will I talk of God while I am sharing my vision (what I plan to do) or following through on it?

   Assumption: Rephrase the vision in explicit theological language to describe how God is at work in it. Without explicit talk of God, Christian mission is incomplete. Proclamation must include word as well as example. These words may not be suitable for use with the non-Christian. However, some non-Christians may be intrigued by the depth of the vision when God is implied, even named.

7. How will I invite others to join me at Jesus' table to be fed and empowered to achieve this vision? (How will I encourage others to seek help in church life?)

   Assumption: The Christian missionary must be part of a Christian congregation. The Word is read and spoken to clarify the purpose and direction of the mission. The Sacrament is shared to receive the power to carry on the mission.

Work through the questions in whatever order works for you. For first users, as you think of one of the fields, what is it you are trying to do right now in that field to make it better? What comes to your mind is your working answer to Question 4 in that field. Write it in and then work your way back to the first question; then work ahead to the last question. Fifteen minutes can be enough to work through the seven questions for a field. Finally, when one mission is completed, be ready to repeat the questions to discern your next mission in that field.

The questions for each mission field

For ease in using this method for mission discernment, the questions for each mission field follow. Copy them as needed and note their source clearly. The parentheses offer alternate wording when desired.

Home

1. What has God been doing or telling me through my life in my home?

2. What conditions inhibit reconciliation, justice, and love (peacemaking, fairness, and caring) in my home?

3. What change is needed to increase reconciliation, justice, and love (peacemaking, fairness, and caring) in my home?

4. What will I do to achieve this change considering my gifts, limitations, and convictions?

5. What vision (description of what I will do) will I use to draw others into working with me for this change?

6. How will I talk of God while I am sharing my vision (what I plan to do) or following through on it?

7. How will I invite others to join me at Jesus' table to be fed and empowered to achieve this vision? (How will I encourage others to seek help in church life?)

Work (includes School and Volunteer Work)

1. What has God been doing or telling me in my daily work/school/volunteer work?

2. What conditions inhibit reconciliation, justice, and love (peacemaking, fairness, and caring) in my daily work / school / volunteer work?

3. What change is needed to increase reconciliation, justice, and love (peacemaking, fairness, and caring) there?

4. What will I do to achieve this change considering my gifts, limitations, and convictions?

5. What vision (description of what I will do) will I use to draw others into working with me for this change?

6. How will I talk of God while I am sharing my vision (what I plan to do) or following through on it?

7. How will I invite others to join me at Jesus' table to be fed and empowered to achieve this vision? (How will I encourage others to seek help in church life?)

The Local Community

1. What has God been doing or telling me in my life in our community (neighborhood or town or city)?

2. What conditions inhibit reconciliation, justice, and love (peacemaking, fairness, and caring) in our local community?

3. What change is needed to increase reconciliation, justice, and love (peacemaking, fairness, and caring) in our local community?

4. What will I do to achieve this change considering my gifts, limitations, and convictions?

5. What vision (description of what I will do) will I use to draw others into working with me for this change?

6. How will I talk of God while I am sharing my vision (what I plan to do) or following through on it?

7. How will I invite others to join me at Jesus' table to be fed and empowered to achieve this vision? (How will I encourage others to seek help in church life?)

The Wider World

1. What has God been doing or telling me in the conditions of our society, culture, economics, or government in our county, or our state, or our nation, or our world?

2. What conditions in our society, culture, economics, or government inhibit reconciliation, justice, and love (peacemaking, fairness, and caring) in our county, or our state, or our nation, or our world?

3. What change is needed to increase reconciliation, justice, and love (peacemaking, fairness, and caring) there?

4. What will I do to achieve this change considering my gifts, limitations, and convictions?

5. What vision (description of what I will do) will I use to draw others into working with me for this change?

6. How will I talk of God while I am sharing my vision (what I plan to do) or following through on it?

7. How will I invite others to join me at Jesus' table to be fed and empowered to achieve this vision? (How will I encourage others to seek help in church life?)

Leisure

1. What has God been doing or telling me in my leisure (my own time, play, or personal growth)?

2. What conditions inhibit reconciliation, justice, and love (peacemaking, fairness, and caring) in my leisure (my own time, play, or personal growth)?

3. What change is needed to increase reconciliation, justice, and love (peacemaking, fairness, and caring) there?

4. What will I do to achieve this change considering my gifts, limitations, and convictions?

5. What vision (description of what I will do) will I use to draw others into working with me for this change?

6. How will I talk of God while I am sharing my vision (what I plan to do) or following through on it?

7. How will I invite others to join me at Jesus' table to be fed and empowered to achieve this vision? (How will I encourage others to seek help in church life?)

Church

1. What has God been doing or telling me through my life in the church (congregation, diocese, or communion — USA or worldwide)?

2. What conditions inhibit reconciliation, justice, and love (peacemaking, fairness, and caring) in the church (congregation, diocese, or communion — USA or worldwide)?

3. What change is needed to increase reconciliation, justice, and love (peacemaking, fairness, and caring) there?

4. What will I do to achieve this change considering my gifts, limitations, and convictions?

5. What vision (description of what I will do) will I use to draw others into working with me for this change?

6. How will I talk of God while I am sharing my vision (what I plan to do) or following through on it?

7. How will I invite others to join me at Jesus' table to be fed and empowered to achieve this vision? (How will I encourage others to seek help in church life?) ✦

Appendix B — A Collection of Insights About Paradigms

George L. Peabody collected these insights about paradigms from the extensive resources available. They are reprinted here with his permission.

Definitions of a paradigm

A set of rules and regulations that:

(1) defines boundaries, and

(2) tells you what to do to be successful within these boundaries. Success is measured in terms of problems solved and situations coped with satisfactorily.

A pattern.

A set of assumptions about reality.

A frame of reference. A way to look at the world. When trapped in a paradigm, we see no other way of seeing things.

Paradigm shift defined

A change in the rules and assumptions. It appears when the prevailing paradigm is still working but solving fewer and fewer problems. Times of paradigm shifting are turbulent.

Paradigm shifter

– Usually an outsider who sees things afresh, or a young person beginning a new discipline, or an older person who has moved to a new discipline.

– A person not invested in the old paradigm which still has a lot of payoff for those who hold it.

– Or a tinkerer who is trying to solve his/her own problem and ends up solving a whole class of problems that were not getting solved by the old paradigm.

The shifter is NOT rewarded.

– The new paradigm puts at risk those who are holding the old one.

– But there is also the opportunity for great benefit for the shifter who can capitalize on getting into it early.

– When you change your paradigm, you are empowered to see by the new rules; to see and to do what you could not do before.

About living with paradigms

People holding different paradigms can observe the same data, but each one simply cannot see what the other sees.

The "paradigm effect": what is perfectly obvious to persons with one paradigm is literally invisible to persons with a different paradigm.

When people have important differences, it can well be because they hold different paradigms. No communication can take place until you can get inside the other's paradigm. That does not mean you have to agree with the other.

To see the future, we must put aside our certainties in the present rules — develop "paradigm pliancy" — and look to people on the fringes who may be creating or exploiting new paradigms. ✦

Appendix C — Discerning Present Concerns and Goals as Missions

This format was developed to orient leaders of a congregation to a vision of the members as the missionaries. It can also be used to orient the rest of the members to see that they, too, are missionaries. Its core is discovering one's present concerns and goals as missions. It can be done in sixty to ninety minutes. It has also been used as preparation for baptism. Children as young as the first grade have participated with their parents and godparents. Adapt the resources that follow as needed.

1. Begin with reading through a page that summarizes the approach. Sample:

   a. God's mission is to preserve good and to overcome evil and bring all humanity and nature to the fulfillment intended at creation.

   b. God's mission has a church. The church does not have a mission. The mission has a church.

   c. Jesus is the center of God's mission to preserve good and to overcome evil and to bring us and all creation back to loving and caring life with God and each other.

   d. Jesus preserved what was good and opened the way to greater good. Jesus struggled with evil and overcame it. He stopped evil in himself. His resurrection is the sign of his victory.

   e. He struggles with evil and preserves and increases good today.

   f. The Holy Spirit helps us to join Jesus and empowers us, too, in the fight against evil and the preserving and increasing of what is good.

   g. Baptism is joining the mission of Jesus to fight against evil and to preserve and to increase good.

   h. Each of us has six fields of mission:

Home and friendships

Work — school for students

Local community

Wider world

Leisure / recreation

Church

i. Baptism ends with communion so each communion repeats our baptism.

j. Sunday worship and communion guide us in how we live and give us the power to live that way. The Bible readings and sermon are mostly about how we live. The prayers and bread and cup are mostly about receiving power to live that way.

k. We will work our way into this vision. Prepare for the baptism of A and B by each of us naming one of our missions.

2. Each person works through these four questions making notes as he or she does.

a. Pick one of the mission fields where you are working to make things better. (All share their choices. Then all return to completing the next three questions on their own.)

b. What are you trying to make better there?

c. What are you working against?

d. What do you want to happen there?

3. All share their answers.

4. Each reflects for a moment on "How might God be at work here (in what I have described)?" and then shares his or her thoughts.

5. Suggest that each person has described one of his or her present missions in one of life's daily arenas.

a. Outline four dimensions of a mission.

i.   A mission is specific.

ii. A mission includes what is to be done to achieve it.

iii. Mission is discerned as what God is calling one to do, to be, or to change.

iv. The duration of the mission may range from brief to ongoing. When the mission is relatively completed, work to discern your new mission in that field.

b. Ask each to comment on what it is like to see this very specific concern or goal as a mission.

6. Summarize and conclude with a restatement of the vision or the congregation's mission statement. ✦

Appendix D — Two Samples: the Vision in a Congregation's Life and Worship

Summaries of the vision and worship may be useful handouts to newcomers and to present members. These handouts may be useful wherever information about the congregation is offered.

Sample 1

Living the Mission at St. John's Episcopal Church

"We all share in God's work of calling, forming, sending, and supporting Christians as agents of love, justice, and peace as shown through the life of Jesus Christ. We seek to live this way in every part of daily life: home, work, local community, wider world, leisure, and church."

How we live the mission

We are rebuilding our congregation for this mission.

We believe Jesus Christ is concerned the most about how we live from Monday to Monday.

We gather on Sunday to learn more about how to live and to receive the power to live what we have learned.

Through the praise, readings, sermon, and prayers, we learn more about how to live as followers of Jesus.

Through the bread and the cup, we receive Jesus' power to live what we have learned.

What guides our living

Jesus is the center of God's mission to overcome evil, to preserve and increase good, and to bring us and all creation back to loving and caring life with God and each other.

- Jesus preserved what was good and opened the way to greater good.

- Jesus struggled with evil and overcame it. He stopped evil in himself. His resurrection is the sign of his victory.

- Jesus struggles with evil and preserves and increases good today. The Holy Spirit helps us to join Jesus and empowers us, too, in struggling against evil and in preserving and increasing good.

In baptism, we join the mission of Jesus to fight against evil and to preserve and increase good. The Holy Spirit gives us the power for this mission. We end baptism with sharing Jesus Christ through the bread and the cup of his table. So each communion recalls our baptism.

Each of us lives out our mission for Jesus in six areas of daily life — in six "fields of mission:" home and friendships, work (includes school and volunteer work), local community, wider world, leisure/recreation, and church.

Also, daily individual prayer and regular biblical reflection in small groups help us to keep ourselves open to receive God's guidance and power.

Sample 2

Sharing the Mission in Holy Communion at St. John's

We believe Jesus Christ is "really present" when we gather around his table.

For us, that is the best way to describe how he is present. We are not at just a memorial service. Neither are we at some miraculous change of the bread and the wine into the actual body and blood of Jesus. We say, simply, "Jesus Christ is really present." It is a middle ground that tries to say what we experience without trying to say too much. We are in the middle between the two.

the bread and wine are a memorial of Jesus Christ

Jesus Christ is really present

the bread and wine become the actual body and blood of Jesus Christ

Holy Communion grew out of the experience of the first Christians.

They found they met Jesus alive and present as they broke bread together. Jesus and the disciples had often dined together. They always said a special blessing over the bread and the wine. At the last supper, Jesus said, "This is my body," as he blessed the bread. As he blessed the wine, he said, "This is my blood." After his death, his followers continued to eat together. When they blessed the bread and the wine, they remembered these words and experienced his presence among them.

What makes the bread and wine special?

We remember in thanksgiving the story of God's work in our behalf from creation, through the call of Israel, to Jesus Christ, to the gift of the Holy Spirit and the call of the church, to the church's work in history to this very moment, and to us here today.

We offer ourselves to be God's co-workers and pray for God to continue the work of overcoming evil and preserving and increasing good with love and justice through us. We reaffirm our baptism in each communion.

An experiential way to talk of Holy Communion:

We need a sign — something we can see and feel as well as hear.

Two analogies:

Eating together expresses, affirms, and deepens our relationships;

We become what we eat — the food becomes part of us.

As we eat the bread and drink the wine in the presence of our risen Lord, we take in his power and ability to cope with evil and to preserve and increase good.

> Adapt these samples to the worship of your communion. Show how worship gives direction and power for daily missions. ◆